"*Black Women, Intersectionality, and Workpla* *Distress* is needed more than ever—right now— ... . complicated world that we live in. Hollis, with her vast expertise on bullying and personal narrative, takes on the challenging topic of bullying as it relates to race and gender. She demonstrates raw emotion and combines it with rigorous research."

Marybeth Gasman, PhD, *Samuel DeWitt Proctor Endowed Chair in Education and Distinguished Professor, Graduate School of Education; Associate Dean for Research, Rutgers, Graduate School of Education, Rutgers University, New Brunswick*

"This book is an education! Centering the voices and experiences of Black women in a variety of work contexts, Dr. Hollis explores their heightened vulnerability to being bullied and harassed. Weaving together relevant social theories with her own empirical research and experiences, Dr. Hollis powerfully illustrates the ways environments and colleagues silence and undermine the recognition and expression of Black women's knowledge, experience, and health to the detriment of all of us. But don't give up hope! Dr. Hollis provides thoughtful guidance on how organizations can challenge and restructure the workplace to fully recognize, engage and benefit from the wisdom and brilliance of Black women and indeed all persons."

Loraleigh Keashly, PhD, *Associate Dean, Curricular and Student Affairs, College of Fine, Performing and Communication Arts; Professor, Department of Communication*

"*Black Women, Intersectionality, and Workplace Bullying: Intersecting Distress* is not only one of the most important books written on workplace bullying. It is one of the only texts that center Black women's experiences with this problematic phenomenon. Utilizing compelling data, Hollis exposes the ineptness of workplace leadership to eliminate work conditions that are hostile and discriminatory. With uncompromising boldness and clarity, she addresses some of its' primary causes such as systemic racism and sexism. She also acknowledges intra-racial and intra-gender issues such as colorism and classism that can be hidden in plain sight. This book is a must read for workplace executives and leaders who are committed to going beyond being reactive to bullying who want to correctly address this issue in their work environment or eliminate it before it starts."

Sydney Freeman, Jr., PhD CFD, COI, SOLC, EMC, *Professor, University of Idaho, Leadership and Counseling Department; Affiliate Faculty of Africana Studies Minor and History; Founder and Director, University of Idaho Black History Research Lab*

"A study mentioned in *Harvard Business Review* on February 1, 2022, found that while 34% of female employees in the study reported workplace harassment, one in four Black women had experienced workplace harassment by a more junior colleague (22%) or that the perpetrator was another woman (23%). A more complex story emerges from this, telling us why taking the intersectional approach to workplace harassment of Black women is critical in seeking solutions. Simplifying workplace bullying and harassment by ignoring the intersecting factors of race, gender, and seniority will succeed only in silencing Black women's voices in the workplace.

Years from now, Leah Hollis' studies in this book will be recognized as a seminal body of work defining a pivotal moment in social justice research on the intersectional approach to workplace bullying and harassment. Prof. Hollis' works tell us what we need to know to build a more just workplace: the *intersection* of gender and race could easily be missed if we were only looking at data related to *singular* identities of race or gender. Prof. Hollis offers us not just words but evidence-based data on how an intersectional approach to workplace bullying of Black women is needed to address how racism, sexism, and power differentials work together to undermine a socially just workplace for all. This book is essential reading for all social sciences scholars and makes a significant contribution to the intersectionality literature."

Daphne Halkias, PhD, *Professor and Distinguished Research Fellow, École des Ponts Business School, Paris*

"Dr. Hollis is one of America's leading experts on the sociological and psychological foundations of the type of bullying that arises from complex intersectional vectors to aggravate Black women scholars in their academic life and career. While injustice in the workplace is not new, and neither is the experience of being subjected to bullying on the job, it is strange that while a higher percentage of Black women than men in America earn the highest academic degrees, the individual experiences of these bullied women in higher education has so rarely been analyzed systematically. This short book presents a history of the problem, the heightened intersectional pressures on Black women scholars that lead to the intensification of the problem, its presence throughout higher education (including in sports and administration as well as on research faculties), and the need for victims to remain vigilant to the always deleterious presence of bullying."

Joseph Drew, PhD, *Editor-in-Chief, Comparative Civilizational Review; Professor, University of Maryland Global Campus*

"Leah P. Hollis has produced a theoretically sound and data-driven high-quality book regarding intersectionality as it pertains to workplace bullying in higher education. Based on an abundance of data, the book provides recommendations regarding ways to address workplace bullying as an aspect of the ongoing pursuit of equity and social justice. Hollis' book is an essential reading for staff, faculty, administrators and students in higher education."

Jack L. Daniel, PhD, *Vice Provost and Professor Emeritus, University of Pittsburgh*

"Dr. Hollis's work is a thoughtful series of research arguments that provokes the reader to consider the role of multiple identities targeted by workplace bullying. Though anyone can face bullying, this volume privileges Black women and the complex socially constructed intersection of race and gender that Black women embody. This empirical research is a call to arms for those committed to social justice and equity."

Jennifer Swann, PhD, *Professor, Ombudsperson, Lehigh University*

Black Women, Intersectionality, and Workplace Bullying

Black Women, Intersectionality, and Workplace Bullying extends and enriches the current literature on workplace bullying by examining specifically how work abuse disproportionality hurts women of color, affecting their mental health negatively and hence their career progression.

In this interdisciplinary text, Hollis combines the fields of intersectionality and workplace bullying to present a balanced offering of conceptual essays and empirical research studies. The chapters explore how researchers have previously used empirical studies to address race and gender before arguing that the more complex an identity or intersectional position, such as being a Black gender fluid woman, the more likely a person shall experience workplace bullying. The author also looks at how this affects Black women's mental health, such as through increased anxiety, depression, insomnia, and self-medicating behaviors, before looking specifically at Black female athletes as a study, the topic of colorism at work and its impact on Black women, and how workplace bullying compromises organizations diversity and inclusion initiatives.

This book will be of immense interest to graduate students and academics in the fields of social work, ethnic studies, Black studies, Africana studies, gender studies, political science, sociology, psychology, and social justice. It will also be of interest to those interested in intersectionality and how this relates to race and gender of women.

Leah P. Hollis, a visiting professor at the Samuel Dewitt Proctor Institute at Rutgers University, is a noted expert in workplace bullying. She received her Doctor of Education as a Martin Luther King, Jr. Fellow from Boston University.

Leading Conversations on Black Sexualities and Identities
Series editors: James C. Wadley

Leading Conversations in Black Sexualities and Identities aims to stimulate sensitive conversations and teachings surrounding Black sexuality. Written by academics and practitioners who have dedicated their work to the distinctive sexual and relational experiences of persons of African descent, the series aims to provoke an enhanced understanding throughout the field of sexology and identify educational and clinical strategies for change. Amplifying issues and voices often minimalized and marginalized, this series is a continuation and expansion of inquiry and advocacy upon the complexities and nuances of relational negotiation, identity affirmation, critical discourse, and liberated sexual expression.

Titles in the series:

Black Women, Intersectionality, and Workplace Bullying

Intersecting Distress

Leah P. Hollis

Routledge
Taylor & Francis Group

NEW YORK AND LONDON

First published 2022
by Routledge
605 Third Avenue, New York, NY 10158

and by Routledge
4 Park Square, Milton Park, Abingdon, Oxon, OX14 4RN

Routledge is an imprint of the Taylor & Francis Group, an informa business

© 2022 Leah P. Hollis

Library of Congress Cataloging-in-Publication Data
A catalog record for this title has been requested

ISBN: 978-1-032-03534-5 (hbk)
ISBN: 978-1-032-03539-0 (pbk)
ISBN: 978-1-003-18781-3 (ebk)

DOI: 10.4324/9781003187813

Typeset in Times New Roman
by Newgen Publishing UK

Contents

Foreword

I believe it was about ten years ago that I met my colleague, Leah Hollis. When we first talked, I was privileged to share with her some of the challenges that some Black women experience in the academy with not being valued and being bullied. I was saddened to hear stories about some of our mutual colleagues who had to navigate difficult systemic structures that were impediments to their professional positions and trajectory. Leah and I have had many conversations over the years about how her research has explored and unpacked some of the adverse experiences of Black women at colleges and universities; their resilience in the face of harassment and bullying; and the strategies they employ to navigate complex social settings and the identities (e.g., race, gender, socioeconomic status, sexual identity) they maintain. Usually, our discussions focus on power inequities, white patriarchal systems of oppression, inadequate supportive resources, and how it is sometimes difficult for professionals to process conflicting feelings about themselves and their places of employment. I must say that I really enjoy these honest conversations with Leah as allow for critical thinking, reflection, and pride in our work.

I was extremely happy that Leah was interested in participating in this initiative.

For the third installment of *Leading Conversations about Black Sexualities and Identities*, Leah Hollis offers us a wonderful and timely collection of empirically driven essays about Black women, intersectionality, and workplace bullying.

What's compelling about this contribution to the literature and our community is that she uses some of her own experiences and research to gracefully capture the impact that harassment and bullying have on the identities and relationships that Black women have with themselves and others. What's unfortunate is that even after the #MeToo movement, Black women are still targets for unfair professional policies and practices that dishonor their work. Moreover, sometimes colleagues are complicit and enable Black women to be the recipients and victims of bullying (Salin, 2003). Hollis's research suggests that bullying is on the rise for Black women who attempt to manage other oppressed identities (e.g., low socioeconomic status and/or identify as queer). Without supportive structures and education in the workplace, bullying is likely to continue.

Hollis also purports a history of workplace bullying and has a severe negative effect on Black women. She candidly discusses the role of stress as a product of psychological pressure in the workplace. She found that one-third of a sample of professional Black women at Historically Black Colleges and Universities (HBCUs) indicated that they experienced anxiety attacks; another quarter experienced insomnia, weight problems, and/or depression. Colleges and universities must do more to change their policies so that Black women can feel protected, safe, and valued in these settings. Hollis's work is enlightening and inspirational as all of us are responsible for creating and maintaining spaces for Black women to excel in.

James C. Wadley, Ph.D.
Licensed Professional Counselor (PA & NJ)
Professor, Lincoln University

Reference

Salin, D. (2003). Ways of explaining workplace bullying: A review of enabling, motivating and precipitating structures and processes in the work environment. *Human Relations*, *56*(10), 1213–1232.

Acknowledgment

I am a Black woman scholar. Thus, almost by definition, I too have been subject to some atrocious and inhumane workplace treatment, often by people who look like me.

My choice is to focus on the North Stars of friends and mentors who light the way from the pervasive darkness of workplace bullying that so many of us face.

See your own light and seek your North Star.

1 Strength in Numbers
Collective Voice in Resisting Workplace Injustice

Equity Exordium

Intersectionality studies often invoke Audre Lorde's quote, "The *master's tools* will never dismantle the master's house" (1984). Lorde's comments express that one cannot overcome the discrimination and oppression heaped upon people of color by mimicking the dominant culture. While the BIPOC community should not adopt oppressive strategies the dominant culture uses, the BIPOC community should also claim its tools. So often, math proficiency is assigned to White and Asian scholars. However, the history below shows that mathematical reasoning did not originate with the current dominant culture, but instead its inception is among African counties. Those resisting oppression should know all tools available to them.

Background

History shows people of color that there is the power in numbers. Too often, Black and brown people have been lulled into believing that math, science, and statistics are the province of White men or Asian scholars (Shah, 2019; Trytten, Lowe & Walden, 2012). However, the birthplace of civilization did not just give rise to literature, philosophy, and medicine; math and statistics also found its inception in African civilization. Hence, while Lorde states, "The *master's tools* will never dismantle the master's house" (Lorde, 1984), we need to recognize our own tools in the history and mathematically reasoning that originated in Africa and used continuously throughout the diaspora (Walker & Matthews, 2014).

Thought to be the earliest evidence of any human mathematical tabulations, Africans, in what is now modern Namibia, used the Lebombo Bone 37,000 years ago to keep track of time and moon phases (Walker & Matthews, 2014). Ancient Egyptian

DOI: 10.4324/9781003187813-1

papyrus revealed mathematical and exponential reasoning through hieroglyphics. African scholars, Setati and Bangura (2011), confirm ancient mathematical calculations were found by the Egyptians and the Moors. These people designed objects such as drums, spears, masks, combs, and canoes to have a geometrical symmetry to make them functional (Setati & Bangura, 2011). Further, medieval mathematical arts were used in universities in Timbuktu and Katsina. In fact, a Greek philosopher Aristotle recognized Egypt as the "cradle of mathematical arts" (Walker & Matthews, 2014). Other branches of mathematical reasoning such as geometry and astronomy are part of the Rhind Mathematical Papyrus, now in the British Museum (Walker & Matthews, 2014).

Ancient Egyptian records show that Africans were using mathematical proofs in agriculture and industry; they also used fractions, multiplication, and division to manage the spoils of war, livestock and grain. Advanced mathematical reasoning in algebra and geometry was also common in Egyptian life. Hence, their sophisticated mathematical reasoning culminated in the great pyramids of Giza, numerous monuments, and advanced monitoring of the stars.

Across the African continent, other cultures utilized advanced numerical and mathematical systems. Math was used in the Ghana region in 900 AD; research shows that the Ashanti tribe of the 18th and 19th centuries used math in their day-to-day lives. Mathematician Zaslavsky (1973) confirmed a Yoruba counting system that had been used for four centuries. She also uncovered an ancient Ethiopian mathematical board game dating back to 700 BC. Kings rising to power used this tactical game using two rows and six holes each as part of their rites of passage process to prove their worthiness and superior stratagem; winning the game meant that the rising king could outwit adversaries (Walters & Matthews, 2014; Zaslavsky, 1973).

Similarly, the Kuba Kingdom in the Congo used mathematical games such as gambling, a statistical game of chance; the Songhai Empire had a mathematical game known as Sudanese chess. The Igbo nation is often considered one of the most intellectually advanced cultures (Chisala, 2015), using mixed mathematics, and linguistics (Umeh, 1998). Further, 16th-century artifacts confirm that the Benin region in Nigeria incorporated mathematical and geometrical reasoning into their textiles, otherwise known as the Benin Bronzes (Crowe, 1971). The African mathematical uses were also noted by Lumpkin (1987), who found that the Angolan culture used complex drawings and algorithms to determine topography. These early cultures were at the inception of the Pythagorean theorem. Other African cultures in Ethiopia, the

Congo, Djenne, Mali, Songhai, and Zimbabwe commonly used math in their day-to-day lives (Walters & Matthews, 2014).

Despite the rich history of Africans developing and using math, contemporary Blacks often claim math anxiety and show poor performance in math (Hall et al., 1999). These disparities in math performance between White and Black students have led to fewer Black students pursuing math majors in college (Husni, 2006). Consequently, the Black community often avoids math, thereby turning its back on intellectual processes belonging to our community. The fight for civil rights needs to embrace all tools in our toolbox. Several scholars in Kaye and Aickin's (1986) anthology prove that math and statistics are viable tools in establishing disparate impact, jury selection, and a host of unconstitutional acts. Consequently, the Black community needs to reclaim its mathematical history and reasoning in the ubiquitous fight for social justice in our communities.

Power to Corner the Bull

With #MeToo and #BlackLivesMatters movements built and fueled by collective voices raising up to protest, women are questioning unfair practices in the tenure and promotion process. Additionally, Black women specifically are only 2% of all full-time faculty (NCES, 2018). One may contemplate how a discussion on tenure and promotion is related to workplace bullying in higher education. Academic leaders are traditionally promoted from the faculty. A scholar earns tenure, then is promoted to full professor, which leads to the eligibility for academic leadership positions such as dean, assistant vice president, and provost.

Also, by definition, workplace bullying is based on a power differential (Carbo & Hughes, 2010; Rockett et al., 2017). For example, the subordinate person, an assistant professor, does not have the power to bully the dean or the provost. The award of tenure for deserving Black women academics closes the power differential and puts those Black women in a better position to resist maltreatment. When women are denied rightful promotion, they remain under the tyrannical practices of their organization.

Truth in Numbers

In a recent audit of one research institution where women academics were strategizing on how to deal with a misogynist culture, the women identified inconsistent tenure decisions as a salient problem. At Ibhere A&M University (IAMU), women faculty were questioning why so many men, with diminished credentials, were granted tenure and awarded promotions to full professors. This strategy aligns with Kaye and Aickin (1986), highlighting the power of statistical analysis in discrimination litigation. For example, the women faculty retold how one of their recently hired colleagues, who had earned tenure at a previous research university, was denied promotion to full professor. However, in the same department, a male professor who had not published in two years prior to his submitted application was promoted to full professor. In comparison, the female colleague had written a book and over 25 articles over the years, but the male who had less than 15 peer-reviewed articles in his career was granted top rank.

Similarly, in another department, but at the same university, a long-standing woman colleague and international leader in her field had applied to full professor twice, only to hear that her work was not relevant or too dated. Her recent publications were not even considered when she appealed to the provost. However, a male colleague with just seven articles, six self-published, ascended the faculty rank ladder from adjunct, lecturer, assistant professor, associate professor, and then granted full professor, all in six years. The academic community was left wondering what he had done in six years that was worthy of such swift ascendance, while the seasoned and internationally respected woman colleague with over 20 years of scholarship was repeatedly denied the same promotion.

When these examples occured in silos, they seem anecdotal or based on personality conflicts. Yet when the women's group united and statistically analyzed such trends across the university, they found discriminatory practices were the institutional rule rather than the exception. Further, their university had no mechanism to address these discriminatory problems.

In their statistical analysis of faculty and gender, IAMU initially considered assistant, associate, and full professors ranks and three different categories. Splitting the data this way reduced the power and the significance of the test. The women remarked that reaching full professor is not relevant because if one is not granted associate professor, the discussion of full professor is moot. The data were retabulated in concert with IAMU's Institutional Research Office to examine if tenure was affected by gender. The data from that analysis of $n = 423$ faculty are presented below. It was tabulated to answer **RQ1:** At IAMU, are men or women more likely to earn tenure? **H1:** At IAMU, men are more likely to earn tenure.

Therefore, hypothesis **H1**, "At IAMU, men are more likely to earn tenure," is accepted at the $p < .05$ level. $X^2 (1, n = 423) = 4.462, p < .035$.

One might ask, if the women of IAMU had these statistics, why did gender discrimination occur with women across the board. While

Table 1.1 Gender and tenure appointment at IAMU[a] (*n* = 423)

	Yes	No	Total
Men CT	138	93	231
Men Exp CT	127.2	103.8	231
Women CT	95	97	192
Women Exp CT	105.8	86.2	192

Note
a IAMU is a pseudonym.

they had the statistical proof, they did not coordinate collective power. Arguably, whether a group of women come together to resist discrimination, or an individual builds her own collective network, it takes numbers, collective power, and persistence to exact justice.

Collective Resistance

When Rosa Parks sat down on that Montgomery, Alabama bus in December 1955, she had the collective power of the NAACP behind her (Dreier, 2006). After Parks' arrest, Alabama State College instructor JoAnn Robinson and two of her students circulated 35,000 leaflets to the Black community calling for the bus boycott (Mcghee, 2015). As a result, the bus company lost 70% of its ridership. The historical result was a Black community boycotting the bus company for 381 days in a fight to end Jim Crow laws about segregated seating. In June 1956, the City of Birmingham lost to a three-judge panel that ruled that segregation was unconstitutional. After the bus company lost $750,000 (Mcghee, 2015) and the Supreme Court decision, which upheld the lower court decision that segregating the bus was unconstitutional under the 14th Amendment, the boycott ended. Fully integrated buses were put in service, yet the bus company never regained its previous patronage (Mcghee, 2015; Montgomery Advisor, 1956).

At times, a single brave woman initiates a David and Goliath fight in the form of her own legal team. A great example is Lilly Ledbetter fighting the misogynist environment and unequal pay at Goodyear Tire and Rubber Corporation in Gadsden, Alabama. Ledbetter was one of a few women who advanced to a supervisory role; in turn, she was the target of sexual harassment and a continuously hostile environment (Ledbetter & Isoom, 2012). She wrote,

One old-timer who'd been there for forty years was so enraged when I was made supervisor that he immediately requested to be transferred ... another old man flat out announced, "I take orders from a b*tch at home, and I'm not taking orders from a b*tch at work."

(Ledbetter & Isoom, 2012, p. 71)

Despite these problems, Ledbetter soldiered on. She was a supervisor on the night shift and often accustomed to receiving occasional anonymous notes when she emerged from the plant at morning's light. On one occasion, a note was mixed in with her company mail. It had her salary, exactly to the dollar, and the names and salaries of three other tire-room supervisors, all of whom were men who started with the company in 1979 with her (Ledbetter & Isoom, 2012).

The pathway to justice was long and rocky, like most legal battles. Many of her colleagues and friends stopped talking with her, though she had nothing wrong. Nonetheless, Ledbetter had one friend in the company who supported her, along with a union representative at Goodyear. Her husband, Charlie, supported her when she initiated an Equal Employment Opportunity Commission (EEOC) investigation through their Birmingham office. Ledbetter received her right to sue from the EEOC in late 1999 and sought a young attorney, Job Goldfarb, to pursue her claims. A lifetime seemed to lapse between the filing of the lawsuit on November 24, 1999, and January 21, 2003, when the case came to trial (Ledbetter & Isoom, 2012). As the case yawned on, Ledbetter recruited four committed witnesses to support her claims. In this brief description of Ledbetter's journey to court, she mentioned at least nine people, her husband, two attorneys, a union representative, a friend, and four witnesses (Ledbetter & Isoom, 2012). The individual litigant has a collection of people who join in the fight for justice.

Conclusion

Whether through a class action suit, a boycott, or the Black Lives Matter Movement, the power in collective voices has proven to exact change. Unfortunately, legal complaints and civil actions take years, in some cases decades. Complainants must have patience, persistence, and support to proceed between a legal system that moves a glacial speed or a culpable defendant that drags their feet when charged with discrimination. However, one way to ensure that no change occurs is to remain silent.

The years of the COVID-19 pandemic have redirected America's attention to the racial disparities in justice that have occurred over a century. The murders of George Floyd, Ahmaud Arbery, and Daunte Wright at the hands of police have brought unprecedented attention to lethal police brutality. After allegedly trying to pass a fake $20 bill, George Floyd was killed by a Minnesota police officer, Derek Chauvin, who subdued Floyd under his knee for 8 minutes and 46 seconds. Floyd died of asphyxiation and Chavin was convicted of murder (Hutchinson, 2021). A jury found Travis McMichael, Gregory McMichael, and William Bryan guilty in the shooting murder of Ahmaud Arbery (Laughland, 2021). Kim Potter, a woman police officer who mistook her gun for a taser in the death of Daunte Wright was convicted of first- and second-degree murder (Burke, 2021).

These convictions are very different from the 1992 Rodney King beating when all four police officers were caught on videotape in their crime, then acquitted (Chaney & Robertson, 2013). The controversy touched off riots in Los Angeles days after their unjust acquittal. In 2012, the Black community experienced another travesty of justice when George Zimmerman was acquitted of gunning down unarmed 17-year-old Trayvon Martin in Sanford, Florida (Thomas & Blackmon, 2015).

Murders at the hands of police officers in the White community trace back to lynchings of the 1800s and 1900s, through Emmitt Till, Elanor Bumphus, Yusef Hawkins, and Michael Brown. Yet slowly, it appears that the power in collective voice moves the needle toward justice. According to the *New York Times*, 15–26 million people have protested police killings against the Black community, potentially making the Black Lives Matter Movement the largest in American history (Buchanan, Bui, & Patel, 2020). The Pew Research Center reported that two-thirds of Americans support the movement, with 38% of that group strongly supporting the Black Lives Matter Movement (Parker, Horowitz, & Anderson, 2020). In converse, without those voices, society is assured that nothing changes.

Calling for all voices to join against a misogynist and racist behaviors, Bell et al. (2021) recommend a "collective resistance" to challenge individuals and organizations to change to increasingly inclusive paradigms (Contu, 2018; Erskine & Bilimoria, 2019). Black, brown, beige, and White people can foster this change in educating themselves about the injustice facing women and people of color, stretching back to the inception of our country (Hannah-Jones & Elliot, 2019). I join Bell et al. (2021) when they invoke Cooper (1988, pp. 120–121), "The cause of freedom is not the cause of a race or a sect, a party or a class—it is the cause of humankind, the very birthright of humanity."

Reflective Questions and a Look Forward

This chapter documented that mathematical analysis originated in Africa. Further, in the struggle for civil rights and equal protection under the law, aggrieved parties often overlook the power in math and collective voice.

1   Why would one overlook powerful mathematical arguments?
2   How can civil rights activities motivate plaintiffs to embrace numbers (math and collective voice)?
3   What is the weakness in a mathematical approach and how might one overcome that?

Looking forward to Chapter 2, one may consider how intersecting demographic categories are also problematic when fighting for civil rights. For example, is someone facing discrimination because she is Black, a woman, disabled, over 40? What part of her does she have to carve out to stake a claim? Currently, under Title VII, one must state a claim, "because of" harassment, "because of" race, or discriminated against "because of" national origin. Legislation prohibiting workplace bullying would transcend the need to define which category provoked the maltreatment legally. Harassment, discrimination, and other workplace abuse should be banned because it is just inhumane.

References

Bell, M. P., Berry, D., Leopold, J., & Nkomo, S. (2021). Making Black Lives Matter in academia: A black feminist call for collective action against anti-blackness in the academy. *Gender, Work & Organization, 28*, 39–57.

Buchanan, L., Bui, Q., & Patel, J. (2020). Black Lives Matter may be the largest movement in US history. *The New York Times*. www.nytimes.com/interact ive/2020/07/03/us/george-floyd-protests-crowd-size.html

Burke, M. (2021). Juror in Kim Potter trial speaks about how jury found ex-officer guilt of Daunte Wright's Death. *NBC News*. www.nbcnews.com/ news/us-news/juror-kim-potter-trial-speaks-jury-found-ex-officer-guilty-daunte-wrig-rcna10338

Carbo, J., & Hughes, A. (2010). Workplace bullying: Developing a human rights definition from the perspective and experiences of targets. *WorkingUSA, 13*(3), 387–403.

Chaney, C., & Robertson, R. V. (2013). Racism and police brutality in America. *Journal of African American Studies, 17*(4), 480–505.

Chisala, C. (2015). The IQ gap is no longer a black and white issue. The Unz Review. A collection of interesting, important, and controversial perspectives largely excluded from the American mainstream media. www.unz.com/arti cle/the-iq-gap-is-no-longer-a-black-and-white-issue/

Contu, A. (2018). "… the point is to change it"—Yes, but in what direction and how? Intellectual activism as a way of "walking the talk" of critical work in business schools. *Organization*, *25*(2), 282–293.

Cooper, A. J. (1988). *A voice from the south by a black woman of the south.* Oxford University Press.

Crowe, D. W. (1971). The geometry of African art I. Bakuba art. *Journal of Geometry*, *1*(2), 169–182.

Dreier, P. (2006). Rosa parks: Angry, not tired. *Dissent*, *53*(1), 88–92.

Erskine, S. E., & Bilimoria, D. (2019). White allyship of Afro-Diasporic women in the workplace: A transformative strategy for organizational change. *Journal of Leadership & Organizational Studies*, *26*(3), 319–338.

Hall, C.W., Davis, N.B., Bolen, L.M., & Chai R. (1999). Gender and racial differences in mathematical performance. *The Journal of Social Psychology*, *139*(6), 677–689.

Hannah-Jones, N., & Elliott, M. N. (Eds.). (2019). The 1619 project. *New York Times*. www.nytimes.com/interactive/2019/08/14/magazine/1619-america-slavery.html?mtrref=www.google.com&gwh=A0C0E609DDA3B60034630 E11E245C6E3&gwt=pay&assetType=PAYWALL

Husni, M. M. (2006). *Measuring the effect of anxiety reduction techniques on math anxiety levels in students enrolled in an HBCU college* (Order No. 3246016). Available From ProQuest Dissertations & Theses Global (305306571).

Hutchinson, B. (2021). Derek Chauvin wants to go to federal prison, even though it means he'll do more time. *ABC News*. www.theguardian.com/us-news/2021/nov/24/ahmaud-arbery-verdict-guilty

Kaye, D. H., & Aickin, M. (1986). *Statistical methods in discrimination litigation.* Taylor & Francis Group.

Laughland, O. (2021). Ahmaud Arbery verdict: Three white men found guilty of murdering black man as he jogged. *The Guardian*. www.theguardian.com/us-news/2021/nov/24/ahmaud-arbery-verdict-guilty

Ledbetter, L., & Isoom, L.S. (2012). *Grace and grit: My fight for equal pay and fairness at goodyear and beyond.* Penguin Random House.

Lorde, A. (1984). *Sister outsider: Essays and speeches.* Crossing Press.

Lumpkin, B. (1987). *African and African American contributions to mathematics.* US Portland Public Schools.

Mcghee, F. (2015). The montgomery bus boycott and the fall of the montgomery city lines. *The Alabama Review*, *68*(3), 251–268. https://doi.org/10.1353/ala.2015.0020

Montgomery Advertiser. (1956). December 18, 1956; Montgomery Advertiser, November 17, 1956.

National Center on Educational Statistics (NCES). (2018). Race/ethnicity of college faculty. https://nces.ed.gov/fastfacts/display.asp?id=61

Parker, K., Horowitz, J., & Anderson, M. (2020). Amid protests, majorities across racial and ethnic groups express support for the Black Lives Matter movement. The Pew Center. www.pewresearch.org/social-trends/2020/06/12/amid-protests-majorities-across-racial-and-ethnic-groups-express-support-for-the-black-lives-matter-movement/

Rockett, P., Fan, S. K., Dwyer, R. J., & Foy, T. (2017). A human resource management perspective of workplace bullying. *Journal of Aggression, Conflict and Peace Research*, *9*(2), 116–127. https://doi.org/10.1108/JACPR-11-2016-0262

Setati, M., & Bangura, A. K. (2011). *African mathematics: From bones to computers*. UPA Acquisitions Department.

Shah, N. (2019). "Asians are good at math" is not a compliment: STEM success as a threat to personhood. *Harvard Educational Review*, *89*(4), 661–686, 702.

Thomas, A. J., & Blackmon, S. K. M. (2015). The influence of the Trayvon Martin shooting on racial socialization practices of African American parents. *Journal of Black Psychology*, *41*(1), 75–89.

Trytten, D. A., Lowe, A.W., & Walden, S. (2012). "Asians are good at math. What an awful stereotype": The model minority stereotype's impact on Asian American engineering students. *Journal of Engineering Education (Washington, D.C.)*, *101*(3), 439–468. https://doi.org/10.1002/j.2168-9830.2012.tb00057.x

Umeh, A. (1998). *After God is Dibia*. Africa World Press.

Walker, R., & Matthews, J. (2014) *African mathematics: History, textbooks and classroom lessons*. Reklaw Education Limited.

Zaslavsky, C. (1973). *Africa counts*. Lawrence Hill.

2 Bullied Out of Position

Black Women's Complex Intersectionality, Workplace Bullying, and Resulting Career Disruption

Equity Exordium

The year 2021 included the passing of intersectionality scholar and pioneer, bell hooks. Nonetheless, her dedication to Black women's rights, within her commitment to human rights, will be studied for decades. Taking her place among amazing women writers such as Zora Neale Hurston, Octavia Butler, and Maya Angelo, hooks has always reminded all readers that Black women have always resisted systematic oppression from the margin. Her quote, "No other group in America has so had their identity socialized out of existence as have Black women," (1981) remains emblematic of the indelible struggle against interlocking factors that attempt to silence Black women. Trust: hooks' voice and intellect will ring loud through those continuing their counter-hegemonic scholastic equipoise.

Background

The social contract is woven of a fabric originally excluding the current American minority–majority. The Declaration of Independence's primary author, Thomas Jefferson, borrowed directly from Locke's *Second Treatise* (Jayne, 1997). While embracing this British philosophy, Jefferson envisioned a society that privileged male property owners.

> The social contract story yields several morals. First, it implies that private citizens are not the mere chattels of their rulers; they are not slaves or emancipated minors or inferiors by nature. Rather, they are self-determining agents … through an exercise of their own wills.
>
> (Lomasky, 2011, p. 50)

DOI: 10.4324/9781003187813-2

In turn, this philosophy originally denied Native Americans, African slaves, and women the right to self-determination. As the country has evolved, American society has modified public policy to stretch this social contract fabric attempting to include those initially disregarded. Jefferson's constitutional ideals have been updated with the 13th Amendment abolishing slavery in 1864, the 14th Amendment calling for equal protection under the law in 1868, the 15th Amendment in 1870 giving male citizens the right to vote regardless of race, and the 19th Amendment in 1919 for women's right to vote (US Const. amend. XIII, XIV, XV, & XIX). Notably, the 1979 Equal Rights Amendment was three states short of ratification in its attempt to grant women equal rights within the US Constitution. Other federal legislation such as Title VII (1964), the Americans with Disabilities Act (1990), and the Equal Pay Act (2009) attempt to provide that elusive "justice for all."

Frederick Douglass foretold in his 1857 West Indian Emancipation Speech that those in power are reluctant to relinquish such power.

> If there is no struggle there is no progress ... This struggle may be a moral one, or it may be a physical one, and it may be both moral and physical, but it must be a struggle. Power concedes nothing without a demand. It never did and it never will.
>
> (Douglass, Kindle Locations 21621–21625, 1892)

This prophetic message remains applicable to contemporary power struggles for women's rights, racial equity, and voting rights. The social contract requires contentious modifications to protect the marginalized positions of race and gender. Nonetheless, those seeking a fair application of the social contract often find abuse, resistance, and admonishment from hegemonic structures reluctant to release their powerful grip.

Within higher education, a pathway often used to create social equality (McCluskey, 1999), power structures maintain the cultural norms that protect exclusionary traditions. Despite a call for diversity, women and people of color remain underrepresented in higher education. The American Council on Education recounted that women earn more than 50% of all doctoral degrees, but women held only 31% of the full professor positions in 2014 (Johnson, 2016). Further, women faculty members make approximately $15,000 less than their male counterparts, regardless of discipline. These issues are more severe for women of color as Black women make $.63 on the dollar compared to White men, and Hispanic women earn $.54 on the dollar compared to White men (Johnson, 2016).

Within the power structures that erode opportunity for disenfranchised groups, I argue that workplace bullying is a compelling element in higher education that destroys self-determination and career progression for those in marginalized positions. Some researchers have considered the constrained choice, that is, the tough life and career choices that face women who simultaneously seek career advancement (Broadbridge, 2010; Hakim, 2002). Further, Hollis (2016a) shows that as women climb the career ladder and seek promotion, supervision, budgetary responsibilities, and tenure, they are more likely to report being the targets of workplace bullying.

Collins (2019) and Mirza (2015) also utilized Black feminist theory and the backlash women experience within the dominant culture that shapes experiences for female academics with multifaceted identities. While the aforementioned amendments and legislation should have presumably granted more access, many are still excluded from "… life, liberty, and the pursuit of happiness." Therefore, the following data-driven analysis of workplace bullying in higher education gives insight into how those with complex intersectionality are deterred by bullying which denies equity granted to all, but still denied to some.

Theoretical Frame

Symington (2004) noted that intersectionality analysis is a product of women of color scholars in the 1970s who insisted that the identity of women could not be fully considered by isolating one position without the inclusive consideration of the whole person. Legal scholar Kimberlé Crenshaw (1989) introduced the term itself in the late 1980s (Yuval-Davis, 2006). Crenshaw argued that Black women are not simply the subject of racism, or the target of sexism, but instead both forms of discrimination collide in the lives and experiences of Black women. However, racism and sexism are not the only demographic markers that potentially intersect for Black women striving through the dominant culture. Unfavorable class, sexual orientation, religion, language, national origin, and identities potentially outside of the mainstream are positions that can keep women of color locked out of opportunity (Smith, 2013).

Employees from society's marginalized positions often do not have the dominant culture's organizational power and executive rank in higher education. Consequently, the marginalized endure compromised self-determination and often make choices that align with the need for safety instead of the goal of advancing. As a result, the quest to seek terminal degrees, tenure, and career advancement is compromised (Hollis,

2016b). According to Mithaug (1996), self-determination is an inalienable right. However, those with power have access, while those with minimal power have compromised access to this right. To create equitable access to self-determination, "all societies optimize prospects for self-determination for [the] least advantaged members by increasing their capacity and improving their opportunity to self-determine" (Mithaug, 1996, p. 11).

Intersectionality is a complex amalgam of identities, which extends from elements such as race, age, language, culture, sexual orientation, and religion (Center for Women's Global Leadership, 2001). The multiplicity of these identities yields obstructions to "empowerment and advancement" (Center for Women's Global Leadership, 2001, p. 1). Further, a theoretical lens that considers intersectionality recognizes that these identities are not mutually exclusive (Australian Human Rights and EOC, 2001), a point made in the seminal work *Ain't I a Woman* (hooks, 1981). The intersection of race and gender, along with other identities a singular person may embody, must be simultaneously analyzed, instead of parsed apart, or dissected into specific categories. For example, just as a Black woman with a disability proceeds through her life path with several identities simultaneously, the holistic approach to analyzing her positionality should be inclusive of all three demographic markers: Black, woman, and disabled. Therefore, intersectionality "addresses the manner in which racism, patriarchy, class oppression, and other discriminatory systems create inequalities that structure the relative positions of women, races, ethnicities, classes and the like" (Center for Women's Global Leadership, 2001, p. 1).

Brah and Phoenix (2004) wrote that the complexity of race, gender, and social class informs a more complex social position. Their comments align with Andersen (1996), who extends West's discussion (1993) regarding race matters. "Actually, class, gender and race matter, and they matter because they structure interactions, opportunities, consciousness, ideology and the forms of resistance that characterize American life ..." (Andersen,1996, ix). Race, class, and socioeconomic status cannot be relegated to neatly define categories that are analyzed in isolation (McClintock, 1995).

Workplace bullying within this context is potentially the product of many positions embodied by the target, not a singularity of identity. Previous research elucidates how workplace bullying is based on a power dynamic (Hodson, Roscigno, & Lopez, 2006; Hoel & Salin, 2003; Hollis, 2016a). The person with more power controls the dominant culture and sets the stage for access, fairness, and career advancement. Looking at workplace bullying with a perspective on intersectionality acknowledges that targets may be harassed for several identities experienced by one person. Hence, Samuels and Ross-Sheriff (2008) stated that researchers should proceed with this understanding, that there is a "myriad [of] overlapping and mutually reinforcing oppressions that many women face in addition to gender. It is no longer acceptable to produce analyses that are embedded solely within an essentialist or universal collective experience as 'woman'" (p. 5).

Problem Statement

The literature on intersectionality shows a need to consider the multifaceted positionality of women, instead of dissecting their personas creating mutually exclusive categories of race, gender, age, religion, culture, and sexual orientation. Further, the body of literature on workplace bullying emerging from seminal scholars of Northern Europe typically analyzes a population that is comparatively more homogenous than the diverse American populations (Einarsen, Hoel, Zapf, & Cooper, 2010; Glasø, Matthiesen, Nielsen, & Einarsen, 2007; Rayner & Hoel, 1997).

In addition, even previous American studies have not tackled how increasing intersectionality may be a contributing factor in the targets' propensity to experience workplace bullying. Hence, this analysis considered the complexity of intersectionality and whether such increasing complexity increases the likelihood that a target faces harassment and abuse in the workplace. I have conducted my research by studying the following research questions.

> **Research question #1.** Will the reported experience with bullying increase as the target's intersectionality becomes increasingly compounded?
> **Research question #2.** Will the reported experience with vicarious bullying increase as the target's intersectionality becomes increasingly compounded?

Purpose Statement

Previous studies have shown that the frequency of workplace bullying in higher education is higher than reported workplace bullying in the general American working population (Hollis, 2016a). In a sector that has become increasingly competitive with fewer full-time tenure-track positions (Hollis, 2015) and continuous budget cuts (Mitchell, Palacios, & Leachman, 2014), those facing bullying and abuse may leave the higher education sector. The loss of diverse faculty and staff cripples the educational mission of an increasingly diverse educational system. Therefore, the purpose of this study is to consider the intersectionality of targets that face workplace bullying and consider if increasingly complex positionality increases the likelihood that targets face bullying on the job.

Research Methods

If race is America's birth defect (Fluker, 2008), then the intersectionality of race, gender, and sexual orientation becomes the nation's foster child, frequently disadvantaged and overlooked. Hence, those from multiple marginalized positions often face more intense oppression. McCall (2005) has noted that studying intersectionality can pose complex methodological questions. Often qualitative methods such as ethnographic and phenomenological approaches bring forward the respondents' voices, potentially aligning with social justice thinking that is more inclusive and holistic. The complexity within intersectionality presents a challenge for researchers striving to pinpoint the experiences and positions of women of color (McCall, 2005). Therefore, this research method aligns with Else-Quest and Hyde's (2016) recommendation for quantitative research to embrace the dynamic and interconnectivity of women.

This methodological approach, while primarily quantitative, will use a statistical analysis to illustrate that women of color are increasingly targeted for workplace bullying and harassment as their intersectionality becomes more complex. The larger data set in turn makes these findings plausibly more generalizable, though I would not make the claim that any single study could universally represent the complexities of women's experiences of marginality.

Therefore, this study will utilize a data set, $N = 669$, from a nationwide data collection conducted via SurveyMonkey™ in late 2017/early 2018 to examine the central research question: *What is the likelihood of facing bullying as one's intersectionality becomes more complex?* The sample was based on faculty and staff who were printed in the Higher Education Publications, a directory of higher education professionals. The sample included four-year schools, two-year schools, and professional schools.

A chi-square test was used to examine the prevalence of bullying as the positionality became more complex. First, the frequency of bullying for all participants was considered. Next, the frequency of bullying for women was considered. Third, the frequency of bullying for Black women was considered. The most complex intersectionality considered

was Black women in a religious minority (not Catholic or Protestant).
The following two hypotheses guided this study.

Hypothesis 1 (**H1**): There is an increased likelihood of reportedly
being affected by workplace bullying as the target has increasingly complex intersectionality.

Hypothesis 2 (**H2**): There is an increased likelihood of reportedly
being affected by vicarious workplace bullying as the target has
increasingly complex intersectionality.

Data Collection and Analysis

The specific instrument used to guide this study was developed in 2017
and beta-tested by two professors, a diversity consultant, and two
human resources professionals with experience in higher education.
I used a relay service to distribute the instrument via email to higher
education professionals from October 2017 through the first week of
February 2018. This instrument was sent to potential participants in
all types of higher education institutions. Both four-year and two-year
schools were included in this sample. The resulting sample from this primary data collection was of size $N = 669$.

SPSS IBM was used to conduct the chi-square analysis to determine if the reported experience of workplace bullying increased as the
positionality of the target became more complex. I considered chi-
square tests versus a regression line. A regression shows the strength
of the relationship between bullying and a particular category. The chi-
square will show the likelihood of an association. Given the research
question posed, analyzing the likelihood of the workplace bullying
experience was more relevant than the strength of the relationship.

Findings

Overall, 58% of the higher education respondents reported being
affected by workplace bullying. This is a 4% decline from a recent four-
year study (Hollis, 2015) and a two-year study (Hollis, 2016a). In these
studies, the sample sizes were smaller, yet the same question was asked
via an Internet survey hosted in SurveyMonkey. The slight decline could
be attributed to the increased attention workplace bullying has received
in the American workplace. Further, five states, Tennessee, California,
Utah, and Minnesota, Maryland, and the territory of Puerto Rico have
enacted anti-workplace bullying legislation since the data collection of
the previous two studies (see Table 2.1).

Table 2.1 Respondents affected by workplace bullying

All respondents	58%	386/669
Women	62%	294/473
Black women	68%	52/76
Black women rel[a]	76%	22/29
Black women LGBQ[b]	100%	7/7

Notes
a Note for Black women religion, gender, race, and religion were tabulated.
b Note for Black women LGBQ, gender, race, and gender/sexual minority were tabulated.

Table 2.2 Workplace bullying increased as intersectionality becomes more complex

	All	Wm	Blk Wm	BlkWm Rel	BlkWmLGBQ
Bullied CT	386	295	51	22	7
Bullied Exp	406	288	45	17.6	4.2
Not B CT	283	179	24	7	0
Not B Exp	263	186.3	29.5	11.4	2.8
Total	669	474	75	29	7

To address the central research question, the responses were filtered by demographic information. First, all respondents were tabulated; then women, Black women, and finally Black women who are religious minorities. Also, Black women who are gender/sexual minorities were analyzed (see Table 2.2).

Of all respondents, the actual count of respondents who are affected by workplace bullying is 386, which is 4.9% less than the expected count of 407 for this sample. For all women respondents, 295 reported being affected by bullying, which is 2.4% higher than the expected count of 288 for this sample. For Black women, the actual count was 51, 13% higher than the expected count for this sample, which was 44. For Black women who are also a religious minority, 22 reported being affected by bullying, which is 25% higher than the expected count for this sample, which was 17.6. For Black women who are also gender/sexual minorities, all seven reported being affected by bullying, which is 40% higher than expected for this sample (see Figure 2.1).

Therefore, regarding hypothesis **H1** for this study (there is an increased likelihood of reportedly being affected by workplace bullying as the target has increasingly complex intersectionality), the hypothesis is accepted, $X^2 = (4, N = 669) = 14.67$, $p < .05$, because the chi-square

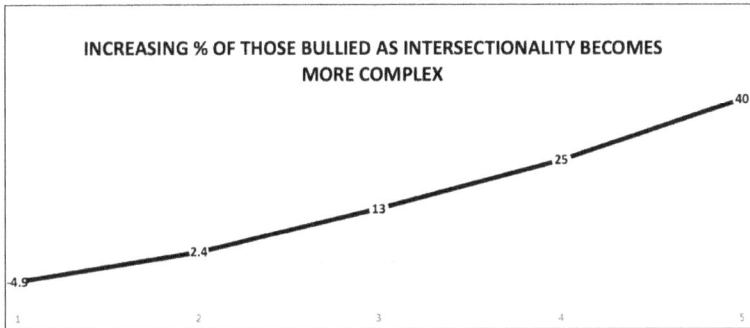

INCREASING % OF THOSE BULLIED AS INTERSECTIONALITY BECOMES
MORE COMPLEX

Figure 2.1 Increased bullying for Black women

Table 2.3 Respondents affected by vicarious bullying

All respondents	42%	283/669
Women	45%	213/473
Black women	54%	41/76
Black women rel[a]	62%	18/29
Black women LGBQ[b]	100%	7/7

Notes
a Note for Black women religion, gender, race, and religion were tabulated.
b Note for Black women LGBQ, gender, race, and gender/sexual minority were tabulated.

test for this sample confirms that as the intersectionality becomes more complex, the likelihood of facing workplace bullying proportionally increases (see Table 2.3).

The second research question addressed if targets with increasingly complex intersectionality are more likely to endure vicarious bullying. Vicarious bullying is an action where the bully sends a subordinate to abuse and harass a third party (Hollis, 2017). A bully may use vicarious bullying when he or she wants to dominate the target or series of targets, but still be viewed as a nice or empathetic person. The vehicle for this style of bullying, or henchman, is typically subordinate to the bully, in need of favor, resources, or political clout. Hence, that person is willing to abuse others in exchange for the bully's favor or influence (Hollis, 2017). The findings show that as a target's positionality becomes increasingly complex, she is also more likely to be the target of vicarious workplace bullying (see Table 2.4).

Table 2.4 Vicarious workplace bullying increased as intersectionality becomes more complex

	All	*Wm*	*Blk Wm*	*BlkWm Rel*	*BlkWmLGBQ*
Bullied CT	283	213	41	18	7
Bullied Exp	357	146	40.5	15.5	3.7
Not B CT	386	60	35	11	0
Not B Exp	312	127	35.5	13.5	33
Total	669	273	76	29	7

Notes
a Note for Black women religion, gender, race, and religion were tabulated.
b Note for Black women LGBQ, gender, race, and gender/sexual minority were tabulated.

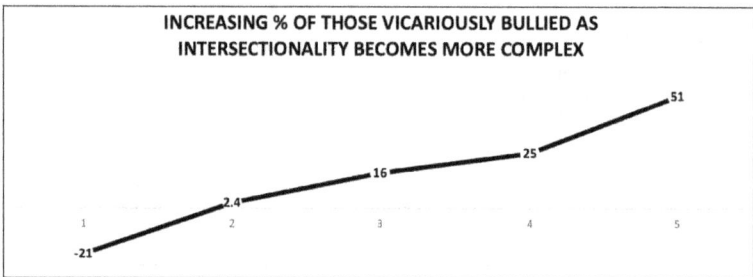

Figure 2.2 Increased vicarious bullying for Black women

For all respondents, the total count of those who are affected by vicarious workplace bullying was 283, which is 21% lower than the expected count of 357 for this sample. Of all women respondents, 295 reported being affected by vicarious bullying, which is 2.4% higher than the expected count of 288 for this sample. For Black women, the actual count was 51, 16% higher than the expected count of 44 for this sample. For Black women who are also a religious minority, 22 reported being affected by vicarious workplace bullying, which is 25% higher than the expected count of 17.6 for this sample. For Black women who are also from the LGBQ community, all seven, or 100%, reported being affected by vicarious bullying, which is 51% higher than the expected count for this sample. Please note the omission of the "T" in this chapter is because no transgender respondents reported their experiences in the survey. (see Figure 2.2).

Therefore, regarding hypothesis **H2** for this study (there is an increased likelihood of reportedly being affected by vicarious workplace bullying

Table 2.5 Open-ended responses from Black women in higher education

---

Respondent #5—I have been in my field for more than 28 years. This is my first job in higher education. I can truly say, I have NEVER seen ANYTHING like what goes on in higher education! I was SO surprised by the behavior! I made the assumption, when accepting this position, that I would be dealing with educated, intelligent individuals. I had no idea the level of bullying that goes on!

Respondent #67—I have never seen Black women work so hard to destroy another woman of color.

Respondent #20—I think the issue of race and gender identity are used to promote certain climates and communities of intolerance. It was interesting how straight and some queer members rally around squeezing me out of my job manipulated the White LGBTQ community.

Respondent #19—I have been in higher ed over 30 years; this is the most vicious place I have worked. Bully is supported by a lying provost—we have no support

Respondent #23—In this TRUMP era, not even HBCUs are safe from bullying and incivility ... esp women.

Respondent#47—Ignored by management when reporting of maltreatment of others. Demoted from job originally hired for and then blocked from being restored to position. Replaced by people who do not even work in this area. Lesser qualified applicant hired to supervise me in my area. I can go on ...

---

as the target has increasingly complex intersectionality), the hypothesis is accepted, $X^2 = (4, N = 669) = 114$, $p < .05$, because the chi-square test for this sample confirms that as the intersectionality becomes more complex, the likelihood of facing vicarious workplace bullying proportionally increases. Further, the questionnaire collected the voices of women with the most complex intersectionality. Their open-ended responses point to the power differential they feel and how the complexity of their positions can make them more susceptible to workplace bullying (see Table 2.5).

Workplace bullying experiences affect Black women's careers, hurting their aspirations to excel in their respective career paths. Black women face unfair demotion, threats of job loss, or changed jobs more often than the rest of the sample because of workplace bullying. Changing jobs to escape a bully hurts job longevity, a quality many employers consider when looking at the stability of a job candidate (see Table 2.6).

These data show that the social contract promises to American citizens fall short in the higher education sector for women with complex intersectionality. While hostility and bullying are behaviors faced by most higher education professionals, this power differential and the resulting intensified abuse disproportionally hurt Black women's careers.

Table 2.6 Adverse career events of Black women compared to the
      remaining sample

	Black women	Remaining sample
Unfairly demoted	54%	32%
Threatened job loss	46%	43%
Changed jobs	48%	25%
Planning to leave	16%	19%
	$n = 74$	$n = 526$

Discussion

Perhaps this examination of workplace bullying deconstructs the experience by examining the frequency of bullying with additional complexities. From the complex interplay of race, gender, and religion (Alinia, 2015), the women's responses in this study highlight the need to continue the struggle for equality in academia and the respective communities from which its scholars emerge.

> Sorting through the layers and levels of oppression and privileges and understanding them collectively without fracturing them as an additive and separate component are crucial if we are to appreciate fully the shared and unique experiences of women as whole beings in their diverse roles and identities [sic].
> (Samuels & Ross-Sheriff, 2008, p. 8)

Further, just as this study is representative of the women in the professional ranks, higher education professionals should consider the impact on the increasingly diverse student body attending higher education. According to estimates from the US census documents of the increasing "minority-majority," by 2020, over half of the nation's children will belong to at least one minority group (DeVore, 2015; US Census, 2015).

Nonetheless, as McBride, Hebson, and Holgate (2015) note, intersectionality is typically not considered in research regarding employee rights, discrimination, and harassment. They offer a call to be more sensitive about intersectionality and recognize that racism, sexism, and classism are not mutually exclusive categories or existing in a binary or ternary system of categories. The findings of this study show that harassment and workplace abuse are increasingly intense for those with unique and complex positionality. From this perspective, the increasingly diverse communities and academic populations cannot just acknowledge, but must further embrace intersectionality, and advocate against power structures to create a modified and more inclusive power structure (Moradi & Grzanka, 2017).

Though some will point to the aforementioned legislation as signs of progress to extend the social contract to all Americans, in practice this social contract has not expanded to address the disenfranchised positions of our community, let alone the amalgam of such positions, to Black women who may be from the LGBT community and/or the member of a religious minority. Yet the conflations of such identities are increasingly prevalent with the majority–minority population expanding and the intersections within such communities increasingly present. The following recommendations are offered to support the increasingly diverse academic community.

Recommendations

1   Higher education human resources professionals should conduct an annual policy audit to confirm if fairness in opportunity, pay, and promotion are occurring in practice and are not just written in the institutional mission statement.
2   Academic affairs can encourage the inclusion of social justice in the curriculum across disciplines.
3   Include a visible and active ombudsman trained in diversity management to hear the concerns of an increasingly diverse academic community. The ombudsman can also tabulate data regarding trends across the university.

While this study may contribute to the conversation on how women face increased harassment and bullying as their complex intersectionality increases, the study could not embody all the potential positions. Roth (2018) challenged scholars to expand beyond Western thought and consider Caribbean, Brazilian, and Middle Eastern perspectives. For example, while this study is based on a large sample, the examination of religious minorities conflated different religious experiences that were non-Western, Hindi, Muslim, and other. For statistical purposes in this study, the counts of non-Western religions were combined to provide introductory insight, but not to suggest that each religion should be melded into the experiences of the others. Therefore, as noted previously, the task of policy makers and human resources is to move beyond compartments, but to consider complexities within the populations served in the application of policy meant to provide social justice.

Reflective Questions and a Look Forward

This chapter captured the fact that as someone's demographic position becomes more complex, the more likely they will face bullying (Women + Black + LGBTQ + etc.). The finding shows that the further away someone is from White and male demographic categories, the more likely they will face some rejection in workplace bullying.

1 As our country evolves into a minority–majority country, how will complex demographics be accepted?
2 How can one apply these dynamics to various races? For example, consider how the findings would be if the race were Hispanic or Jewish.
3 Other studies show that women often bully other women. How might woman-on-woman bullying change how intersectionality is related to bullying?

Looking forward to Chapter 3, a common cliché is, "if you don't have your health, you don't have anything." Nonetheless, society repeatedly has documented the cross-section of poor health, race, and socioeconomic status. Therefore, Chapter 3 embraces Nancy Krieger's Ecosocial Theory which supports how race and the historical moment conflate to produce health disparities for those less fortunate.

References

Alinia, M. (2015). On Black feminist thought: Thinking oppression and resistance through intersectional paradigm. *Ethnic and Racial Studies*, *38*(13), 2334–2340.

Andersen, M. (1996). "Introduction". In E. N.-Ling. Chow, D. Wilkinson, & M. Baca Zinn (Eds.), *Race, class & gender: Common bonds, different voices.* Sage.

Australian Human Rights and EOC (Equal Opportunities Commission). (2001). *HREOC and the world conference against racism.* www.hreoc.gov.au/ worldconference/aus_gender.html

Brah, A., & Phoenix, A. (2004). Ain't I a woman? Revisiting intersectionality. *Journal of International Women's Studies*, *5*(3), 75–86.

Broadbridge, A. (2010). Choice or constraint? Tensions in female retail executives' career narratives. *Gender in Management*, *25*(3), 244–260. doi:10.1108/17542411011036437

Center for Women's Global Leadership (2001). *A women's human rights approach to the world conference against racism.* www.cwgl.rutgers.edu/globalcenter/ policy/gcpospaper.html

Collins, P.H. (2019). The Difference That Power Makes: Intersectionality and Participatory Democracy. In: Hankivsky, O., Jordan-Zachery, J. (eds) The Palgrave Handbook of Intersectionality in Public Policy. The Politics of Intersectionality. Palgrave Macmillan, Cham. https://doi.org/10.1007/978-3-319-98473-5

Crenshaw, K. (1989). Demarginalizing the intersection of race and sex: A Black feminist critique of antidiscrimination doctrine, feminist theory and anti-racist politics. *University of Chicago Legal Forum*, 138–167.

DeVore, C. (2015). Of the four majority-minority states in America, minorities do best In Texas. *Forbes*. www.forbes.com/sites/chuckdevore/2015/06/21/america-majority-minority-by-2044-with-four-states-already-there-minorities-do-best-in-texas/#1335579b287c

Douglass, F. (1892). *The most complete collection of written works & speeches by Frederick Douglass*. (Kindle Locations 21621–21625). Northpointe Classics. Kindle Edition.

Einarsen, S., Hoel, H., Zapf, D., & Cooper, C. (eds.). (2010). *Bullying and harassment in the workplace: Developments in theory, research, and practice.* CRC Press.

Else-Quest, N. M., & Hyde, J. S. (2016). Intersectionality in quantitative psychological research: I. Theoretical and epistemological issues. *Psychology of Women Quarterly*, *40*(2), 155–170.

Fluker, W. (2008). President-elect Barak Obama: Race has been haunting this election. *U.S. News and World Report*. www.morehouse.edu/centers/leadershipcenter/pdf/Fluker_ObamaArticle.pdf

Glasø, L., Matthiesen, S. B., Nielsen, M. B., & Einarsen, S. (2007). Do targets of workplace bullying portray a general victim personality profile? *Scandinavian Journal of Psychology*, *48*(4), 313–319.

Hakim, C. (2002). Lifestyle preferences as determinants of women's differentiated labor market careers. *Work and Occupations*, *29*(4), 428–459.

Hodson, R., Roscigno, V. J., & Lopez, S. H. (2006). Chaos and the abuse of power: Workplace bullying in organizational and interactional context. *Work and Occupations*, *33*(4), 382–416.

Hoel, H., & Salin, D. (2003). 10 Organisational antecedents of workplace bullying. *Bullying and Emotional Abuse in the Workplace*, 203.

Hollis, L. P. (2015). The significance of declining full-time faculty status for community college student retention and graduation: A correlational study with a Keynesian perspective. *International Journal of Humanities and Social Science*, *5*(3), 1–7.

Hollis, L. P. (2016a). *The Coercive Community College: Bullying and its costly impact on the mission to serve underrepresented populations*. Emerald Group Publishing.

Hollis, L. P. (2016b). Socially dominated. The racialized and gendered positionality of those precluded from bullying. *The Coercive Community College: Bullying and its costly impact on the mission to serve underrepresented populations diversity in higher education.* Emerald Group Publishing Limited. doi:10.1108/S1479-364420160000018012

Hollis. L. P. (2017). Higher education henchmen: Vicarious bullying and underrepresented populations. *Advances in Social Sciences Research Journal,* 4(12). 64–73.

hooks, b. (1981). *Ain't I a woman.* South End Press.

Jayne, A. (1997). *Jefferson's "declaration of independence": Origins philosophy and theory.* University of Kentucky Press.

Johnson, H. (2016). *Pipelines pathways, and institutional leadership: An update on the state of women in higher education.* American Council on Education.

Lomasky, L. (2011). Contract convent constitution. *Social Philosophy and Policy Foundation.* doi:10.1017/S0265052510000051

McBride, A., Hebson, G., & Holgate, J. (2015). Intersectionality: Are we taking enough notice in the field of work and employment relations? *Work, Employment and Society,* 29(2), 331–341.

McCall, L. (2005). The complexity of intersectionality. *Signs: Journal of Women in Culture and Society,* 30(3), 1771–1800.

McClintock, A. (1995). *Imperial leather: Race, gender, and sexuality in the colonial contest.* Routledge.

McCluskey, A. T. (1999). Setting the standard: Mary Church Terrell's last campaign for social justice. *Black Scholar,* 29(2/3), 47–53.

Mirza, H. S. (2015). Decolonizing higher education: Black feminism and the intersectionality of race and gender. *Journal of Feminist Scholarship,* (7–8), 1–12.

Mitchell, M., Palacios, V., & Leachman, M. (2014). *States are still funding higher education below pre-recession levels.*Center for Budget and Policy Priority.

Mithaug, D. (1996). *Equal opportunity theory.* Sage.

Moradi, B., & Grzanka, P. R. (2017). Using intersectionality responsibly: Toward critical epistemology, structural analysis, and social justice activism. *Journal of Counseling Psychology,* 64(5), 500.

Rayner, C., & Hoel, H. (1997). A summary review of literature relating to workplace bullying. *Journal of Community & Applied Social Psychology,* 7(3), 181–191.

Roth, J. (2018). Feminism otherwise: Intersectionality beyond occidentalism. *InterDisciplines,* 2.

Samuels, G. M., & Ross-Sheriff, F. (2008). Identity, oppression, and power: Feminisms and intersectionality theory. *Affilia,* 23(1), 5–9.

Smith, S. (2013). Black feminism and intersectionality. *International Socialist Review,* 91, 6–24.

Symington, A. (2004, August). Women's rights and economic change: Intersectionality: A tool for gender and economic justice (No. 9). www.awid.org/publications/primers/intersectionality_en.pdf

US Census. (2015). New census bureau report analyzes U.S. population projections.
www.census.gov/newsroom/press-releases/2015/cb15-tps16.html

US Constitution. Amendments. XIII, XIV, XV, XIX. www.archives.gov/found ing-docs/amendments-11-27

West, C. (1993). *Race matters.* Beacon Press.

Yuval-Davis, N. (2006). Intersectionality and feminist politics. *European Journal of Women's Studies*, *13*(3), 193–209. http://dx.doi.org/10.1177/135050680 6065752

3 Preexisting Intersections

Black Women, Health Issues, and Workplace Bullying

Equity Exordium

In 1993, Joycelyn Elders became the first Black woman to be appointed as the US Surgeon General, serving the Clinton administration. Growing up poor in Arkansas lead Elders to approach health issues within the Black community's health issues with a no-nonsense and realistic approach, devoid of uninformed magical thinking. She is known for her unwavering commitment to truth through quotes like, "Health is more than the absence of disease. Health is about jobs and employment, education, the environment, and all of those things that go into making us healthy." Though her honest and fact-based remarks about health, the AIDS epidemic, and sex education precipitated her untimely resignation from the Clinton administration, Elders remained a force in the Arkansas health community as a professor at the University of Arkansas for Medical Sciences.

Background

My first contemplation of Black women and health came to me as a child, watching a civil rights newsreel at my grandfather's home. I could not have been older than nine but watching this black and white footage of dogs and hoses pummeling Black people shocked, then depressed me. Some of the people were tossed around like those hyped-up gymnastic moves in science fiction movies, just literally blown away. As the newscaster turned back the pages of history, he talked about the cruelty of White southerners visited upon Blacks. A pregnant Black woman was subject to an angry mob who tied her feet, hung her upside down, and then burned her clothes off with gasoline. When the mob discovered that the Black woman was still alive, the ringleader ripped open her pregnant belly with a hatchet and the fetus gave out a quick yelp as it

DOI: 10.4324/9781003187813-3

fell to the ground. The White man crushed the fetus still dangling from her belly with his boot. I learned many years later that this was the heinous killing of Mary Turner from Brooks County, Georgia, a Black woman who protested the lynching of her husband from the prior day (Armstrong, 2011). That story always stuck with me as a cruel reminder of how some White folks totally disregarded Black women's humanity, to the point of shaming her even through a brutal murder.

As grotesquely demonstrated in the 1918 lynching of Mary Turner lynching, discrimination is a health hazard that can lead to mutilation and death. Society can witness firsthand lynching, which has transformed into the mob scenes of the civil rights movement. Moving forward in history, we now see murders of Black citizens at the hands of the police. Police murder is not a new occurrence, but the fact that technology allows people to capture these murders and broadcast them is the new element. What one cannot see, yet experience, is the stress-related and health-harming impact of discrimination and other psychological violence in our workspaces. The erosion of someone's life is not as acute as what we witness on national television but arguably has a similar conclusion of early mortality.

The subtleties of racism and sexism still build up and compromise the health of those subject to such emotional and psychological abuse. Anderson (2010) discussed that such abuse and discrimination have an adverse impact on those who are denied equity and access to work and housing opportunities. Similarly, Bonilla Silva (2010) and Ruscher (2001) confirm that such seemingly understated abuse through verbal and psychological aggression is used to oppress marginalized populations. With the similarity between illegal Title VII harassment and workplace bullying, I add workplace bullying to the "killing me softly" tactics used by dominant cultures and figures to subjugate others.

The history of Black women and work contributes to the health disparities which emerge from harsh and discriminatory working conditions. During slavery, stronger women often endured childbirth in the fields and returned to their work with a child on their back (Stannard, 1992; Taylor, 2020). Under the wicked lash of slave owners, Black women were expected to produce multiple children to enhance a slave master's holdings; consequently, Black women often faced pregnancy every two years (Johnson & Smith, 1999; Taylor, 2020).

Once the 1863 Emancipation Proclamation came and then completed in 1865 with Texas being the last state to comply, hundreds of thousands of slaves were released into the world without food, clothing, shelter, or proper health care. As Downs (2012) confirmed, the emancipation of enslaved people led to a smallpox epidemic. As the formerly enslaved people made their way to freedom, they also encountered dysentery, cholera, pneumonia, yellow fever, and exposure culminating in the largest public health crisis of the 19th century (Downs, 2012).

In this world of abject poverty, starvation, and low wages, Black women often experienced problems securing fair pay from White landowners. As Jones (1985) wrote, many Black women filed grievances about unfair pay. They "were routinely and ruthlessly defrauded of the small amounts they had earned and then run off the place" (Parker, 2004, pp. 45, 54).

Black women who migrated North in the 1890s typically were relegated to agricultural or domestic work. Even if Black women were hired into industrialized jobs, they were still assigned the jobs with the lowest wages (Davis, 1983, p. 88). Into the 1940s, a system emerged analogous to slave auctions. Black women would crowd on street corners every morning, regardless of inclement weather, literally begging to be chosen for work. Often the terms of the work were altered once the women completed the work. White patrons worked Black women longer hours than agreed, extended their duties on a whim, and often paid with clothes or trinkets instead of cash (Davis, 1983). Davis reported on a 1938 article from *the Nation* which chronicled that Black women domestics worked 72 hours a week, "receiving the lowest wages of all occupations" (Lerner, 1977, p. 269). Many live-in Black women domestics toiled on their feet 10–14 hours a day and only saw their families one afternoon a week.

During World War II, the War Labor Board supported equality, yet Congress failed to pass the Women's Equal Pay Act of 1945, the first proposed federal legislation to secure equal pay for women (DuBose, 2017). Unequal pay for women over the decades directly stems from the ideals that women should be apolitical and function in the domestic sphere solely in support of their husbands. Women seeking work at the onset of the industrial age were primarily relegated to textiles, cooking, or cleaning. Black women's unequal pay has a deeper inception born of slavery. Throughout history, Black women were expected to not only work in the house but also to perform heavy duties alongside the men. Black women's work, while necessary, was seldom celebrated or appreciated (Parker, 2004, p. 29).

American history chronicles a stressful work history for Black women. From toiling in the fields to scrubbing toilets, Black women seldom have found peace or appreciation in work. The hazards at work have transformed since slavery through Jim Crow to current working conditions. Our society has created the 1964 Civil Rights legislation which gives women a foundation from which to build a legal battle. Though

Black women have laws available to formally resist discrimination, the legal fight itself protracted and arduous. Additionally, Title VII harassment is defined by its motivation; someone is harassed because of her race, gender, disability or other protected class status. Conversely, workplace bullying is the same behavior, but not overtly attributed to the protected class status. Reflecting on Freire (1972), I argue workplace bullying can be the next step in the evolution of discriminatory behaviors. I do not claim that workplace bullying is exclusively a derivative of discrimination, but I do claim that some workplace bullying is redesigned tyranny and a newer tool for oppressors (Freire, 1972).

Researchers have confirmed that stressful work and living conditions have health-harming consequences for those subjected to such an environment (Kreiger, 2021; Lu et al., 2019). In considering workplace bullying as a true health hazard, I also assert that the negative impact on health because of workplace bullying is particularly severe for Black women. Scholars and writers of years past highlight a salient question about a Black woman's position in American society. Soujourner Truth's 1851 question in her Akron, Ohio speech, "Ar'n't I a Woman?" is still relevant when considering how society dismisses Black women's health concerns. (Mandziuk, 2014). Zora Neale Hurston often stated that Black women were the mules of the earth (Hurston, 1937; Hollis, 2021), dependable, underpaid, overburdened, and overlooked. Over the years, Black women's work environments have not promoted a healthy lifestyle or encouraged self-care. With the historical past and contemporary oppression, Black women constantly encountering these phenomena would remain overstressed and debilitated. Hence, Black women who are at the intersection of race, gender, class, and color, find that their health is compromised in the social milieu that continues to misunderstand her.

Theoretical Frame: Ecosocial Theory

This history informs Kregier (2021) who reminds us that work is not just about an exchange of skills for money. Jobs are accompanied by the psychological and social pressure employees endure to complete the work. These psychological and social pressures include employees' hierarchal occupational status (Kreiger, 2021, p. 85). Those with higher rank and higher pay enjoy a solace found in more prestige and acceptance. In converse, those who face psychological and emotional work hazards such as diminished appreciation and effort-reward imbalance will endure more stress. Kreiger's identification of psychological and emotional hazards potentially aligns with workplace bullying behaviors such as the silent treatment, insults, diminished resources, and stealing one's work. Previous studies confirm that Black women are more likely to be subjected to bullying (Hollis, 2018), and the more complex one's intersectional position, the more likely she will face bullying (Hollis, 2018).

Other studies have also confirmed that constant stress manifests in adverse health problems. Lu et al. (2019) studied telomeres, a biomarker for aging and mortality. "Telomeres are the repetitive sequences of DNA at the ends of chromosomes which protect against DNA degradation" (Lu et al., 2019, p. 33). Their research continues by referring to previous studies which show that stress such as sexism and racism erode the telomere length to the point that telomeres are ineffective in protecting DNA (Calado & Dumitriu, 2013). Lu et al. (2019) also use Clark et al.'s (1999) study and Thompson's (1996) study as a foundation in which racism and discrimination as ubiquitous stressors associated with shorter telomeres. Consequently, shortened telomeres are associated with earlier mortality rates (Sanders & Newman, 2013).

History, race, and class all influence health in what Krieger confirms as the ecosocial approach to understanding health disparities among people of color (Bailey et al., 2017; Krieger, 2021). In reflection, the history of Black women's work in this country starts in 1619, through slavery, reconstruction, and contemporary unequal pay practices that underpay Black women 63% less than White men (AAUW, 2021; Hollis, 2019b). In addition to the demoralizing treatment and unequal pay, scholars note that class is a major variable in seeking health care (Washington, 2006). If a woman has a job that affords her secure living conditions and consistent private insurance, she is better prepared to combat her health issues and that of her children. The example at the time of this writing, COVID-19 as the disproportionately deadly impact on communities of color, shows that poor health is related to class because of the diminished access impoverished people have to quality health care.

Continuing with Kreger's and Lu's logic about chronic stress being associated with health problems and premature mortality, I posit that Black women are susceptible to stress-related health problems related to constant and abusive workplace bullying. Workplace bullying, which can be motivated by racism and sexism (Hollis, 2022), creates traumatic work conditions for the target. Fear of job loss and humiliation suspends targets of workplace bullying in a relentless state of stress. Stress from workplace bullying, just like stress from racism and sexism, jeopardize one's health. As telomeres erode over time, arguably, older Black women would report more health problems as their telomeres shortened under the emotional and psychological stress experienced from workplace bullying.

The Study

The literature and theory confirm that Black women's health is compromised by the ubiquitous stress of being Black and female in a country that has historically disenfranchised both populations. Though the literature confirms the association between discrimination and health issues, this analysis specifically ties workplace bullying experiences in higher education to Black women's health issues. Reasonably, the longer someone is faced with workplace bullying, the more likely that person could develop stress-related health problems. With this in mind, I considered age as the dependent variable to capture the amount of time a target is exposed to workplace abuse.

The Procedure and Resulting Sample

To answer the research questions, I collected data in the spring of 2020 from faculty and collected data from faculty and administrators in the spring of 2018. My survey-based research protocols include developing the survey, which is beta-tested, and then invited respondents via email to engage the survey which is hosted on SurveyMonkey™. From the spring 2020 data collection, 113 Black women completed the three questions required for a multiple regression. Additionally, from the spring 2018 data collection, 68 Black women completed the survey. Therefore, the combination of the spring 2020 sample and spring 2018 sample resulted in 166 Black women who answered the open-ended segment of the study. The respondents' ages range between 23 and 70, with the median age range at 51–60.

Data

This analysis of Black women, health, and workplace bullying is informed by the aforementioned Ecosocial Theory. In short, people are affected by their environments. When such environments produce stress, and such stress emerges from discrimination and harassment, the person facing such stress suffers with health issues. To examine how Black women in higher education are affected by workplace bullying stress in a way that compromises their health, I conducted two analyses. The data set for the multiple regression analysis is from a survey-based data collection from the spring of 2020. I circulated a survey to women faculty at four-year institutions which included three questions that constitute the variables needed for the multiple regression analysis. Age served as the dependent variable. The number of health problems and the coping behaviors were used as the independent variables. Black women were $N = 113$ of the sample collected in the spring. The first research question (**RQ1**) is What is the relationship between the age of the faculty female target and health issues and the resulting coping behaviors in the context of workplace bullying? **H1:** There is a direct relationship between the female targets' age, health problems, and coping behaviors for Black women in higher education.

For this analysis, age served as the dependent variable; the number of health issues is the first independent variable, and the number of coping strategies is the second independent variable.

The second research question (**RQ2**) is How does workplace bullying in higher education affect your health? This analysis is based on a meta-analysis from two samples. The 113 Black women from the 2020 sample and the 53 Black women from a 2018 data collection both were invited to offer open-ended comments about workplace bullying and resulting health issues. From these two samples, 166 Black women faculty and administrators offered their comments which I used in a qualitative content analysis.

Findings

Black women were asked to choose from a list of health problems related to bullying in the question, "Think of your career at HBCUs. Has workplace bullying created health issues? Workplace bullying. (check all that apply)." Because respondents were asked to check all that apply, the percentages do not have a sum of 100% (see Table 3.1).

The multiple regression test, calculated with IBM SPSS version 28, confirmed that the first dependent variable health problems (DV1) are inversely related to age (IV) for Black women dealing with a workplace bully. However, the multiple regression revealed an indirect relation between age (DV1) and coping behaviors (DV2) in response to workplace bullying. In summary, the older the Black woman target, the more coping behaviors she engages because of workplace bullying. Therefore, **H1:** There is a direct relationship between the female targets' age, health problems, and coping behaviors for Black women in higher education is not accepted. These findings are confirmed at a statistically significant level $p < .01$ (see Table 3.2).

A multiple regression was used to calculate the relation between age (DV), impact on age (IV1), coping with bullying (IV2), and health related to bullying. ($F(2, 112) = 3.492$ $p < .034$ with an R^2 of .244 (see Tables 3.3 and 3.4).

Table 3.1 Health issues and coping behaviors for sample (*n* = 113)

Health issues (DV1)		Coping behaviors (DV2)	
Anxiety/panic attacks	32%	Other	17%
Insomnia	27%	Increased insomnia meds	8%
Weight problems	24%	Increased alcohol use	4%
Depression	23%	Increased sedative use	2%
High blood pressure	19%	Increased marijuana use	2%
Skin rashes/hives	14%	Increase tobacco use	2%
Other	12%	Suicide ideation	1%
Reduced libido	7%		
Heart issues	2%		

Table 3.2 Correlation report of age of the Black women targets as an independent variable with coping mechanisms and health of the targets (*N* = 113)

Pearson correlations	Variable
Coping	3.608
Health problems	−.550

Table 3.3 Significance coefficients (*n* = 113)

Included variable	T	Sig.
Coping	1.367	.009
Health problems	.573	.339

Table 3.4 Correlation report of health because of bullying and coping with bullying as independent variable and age as predictor variable (*n* = 113)

		Age	Health	Cope
Pearson correlation	Age	1.00	.010	.228
	Health	.010	1.00	.402
	Cope	.228	.402	1.00
Single tailed	Age	–	.457	.008
	Health	.457	–	.000
	Cope	.008	.000	–

Table 3.5 Health problems for Black women faculty and administrators (*n* = 68)

Trouble sleeping	59%
Sought counseling	40%
Increased alcohol intake	34%
More sedatives	32%
More sleep medication	31%
Decrease interest in physical intimacy	29%
Other	29%
Suicide ideation	4.4%

Qualitative Content Analysis

Before moving on to the qualitative content analysis, I am presenting how the additional Black women from the 2018 data collection report health issues. Sixty-eight Black women answered the survey question about health, "If you have been affected by bullying or cyberbullying any time in your career, how has it affected your health (Choose all that apply)" (see Table 3.5).

The qualitative content analysis regarding Black women and health is based on the sample from 2020 (see Table 3.1) and the sample from 2018 (see Table 3.5). Forty women took the opportunity to further share how workplace bullying adversely affected their health. Though these comments did not emerge as themes, they are still worth mentioning given the severity. Some women mentioned hair loss and vertigo. Other reactions to bullying included a Gran Mal Seizure, heart failure, migraines, fatigue, and admission to the emergency room to deal with the stress. Additionally, the following three themes emerged: #1 seeking personal friends and colleagues for support, #2 practicing mindfulness, #3 women's health issues.

Theme #1 Seeking Personal Support

Under stress, people naturally seek out friends and family for support. In the face of abuse, one can find comfort in speaking with someone who cares. However, the time spent seeking empathetic friends and colleagues is time that neither the target nor the colleague is using to further their work objectives. Respondents' comments about support are below.

"I talk to people outside of work to help me with a script to counter his remarks."

"I seek dinners or calls with supportive friends."

"I cried in the Dean's office from frustration because there was no relief."

Theme #2 Practice Mindfulness

A healthy reaction to bullies is to engage in meditation and mindfulness. By embracing positive elements in an otherwise abuse situation can help people transcend the abuse. For example, one might focus on the clear sky or the birds outside of their window to stay present in positive daily occurrence. Respondents' comments about mindfulness are below.

"I practice mindfulness."
"Use yoga and relaxation techniques."
"Listen to calming and relaxing tones/frequencies."

Theme #3 Women-Specific Health Issues

Just as workplace bullying negatively affects blood pressure and mental health, it also contributes to women-specific health issues. The damage to women's health also can have permanent effects on their children.

"My second child was born a month premature."
"I have irregular menstrual cycles."
"Destroyed family relationships during my kids' childhood."

Discussion

When one considers the research on racism, sexism, stress, and telomeres, the findings which confirm health problems for Black women, especially among older respondents, are consistent with other studies. However, these findings are attributed explicitly to workplace bullying. Consequently, organizations should not relegate workplace bullying to a simple personality conflict, but instead recognize bullying behaviors contributing to the same health-related problems associated with discrimination.

The qualitative and quantitative findings should be read in tandem, meaning regardless of which data is considered first, the two sets of findings complement each other in confirming the negative impact of workplace bullying on Black women's health. These findings also align with the Ecosocial Theory (Krieger, 2021) in which the social environment has a direct and deleterious impact on health. Krieger (2021) considers how environmental stress manifests in health problems as the embodiment of injustice. "Embodiment is at the nexus of con-current and integrated lived realities of health, disease, and well-being in societal and ecological context" (Krieger, 2021, p. 82). I restate this to claim that the intersection of race, gender, social and environmental context manifests in the adverse mental health and compromised well--being for those regularly subjected to abuse. Bullies and their aggressive behaviors abuse less powerful employees, rendering those less powerful people to experiencing stress-related health problems.

Studies have shown that when an environment is saturated with dis-crimination, aggression, and violence (such as during the Jim Crow era), those in that environment experience health problems and higher mortality rates (Krieger et al., 2014). Jones et al. (2007) also stated that extended stress culminates in mental and physical health disorders. Congruently, workplace bullying scholars have empirically tied stressful workplace bullying to depression, insomnia, substance use, post-traumatic stress, and suicide ideation (Hollis, 2019a; Hoopsick et al., 2020; Leach, Poyser, & Butterworth, 2017; Lever et al., 2019; Nielsen et al., 2018; Rodriguez-Muñoz et al., 2020; Spence Laschinger & Nosko, 2015). The Black women respondents for this study reported the same health problems in association with workplace bullying. Consequently, because Black women are disproportionally affected by workplace bullying (Hollis, 2018), Black women reasonably would be more sus-ceptible to health problems and premature mortality resulting from extended exposure to workplace bullying.

Recommendations for Future Study

The literature review and the findings lend themselves to topics for future studies. So often, Black women have minimal representation in a sample. Hence, Black women's health concerns are not prominently studied. Nonetheless, this study confirms that more research is needed on health disparities regarding Black women. Expressly, Black women and health problems stemming from workplace bullying should receive more empirical attention. With the findings in mind, I recommend the following for future study.

Recommendation #1: Mindfulness/Prayer

Black women respondents stated that being mindful and prayerful helps them to withstand workplace bullying. Meditation practices reportedly assuaged the stress from workplace bullying and helped Black women to persevere in toxic workplaces. However, while the findings of this study note meditation practices as a solution, additional empirical research could investigate the amount of time one spends with meditation and if there is an inverse relationship with the perceived intensity of workplace bullying.

Recommendation #2: Colleague/Friends/Bystander Support

The literature on workplace bullying has a gap in how colleagues, friends, and bystanders support bullied people. Further, given the racist and sexist ripple within workplace bullying, Black women are reasonably circumspect with who they can trust. Nonetheless, several women commented that they sought out friends and families for support. In turn, researching colleagues who offer such support would be of further interest in the field. Researchers could examine who Black women trust to share their hostile work experiences. Empirical research could also capture how support systems respond, such as by taking their friend to a counselor, scheduling vacations, or referring bullied friends to other job opportunities.

Recommendation #3: Examine Substance Use and Workplace Bullying

People use substances to manage stress, fall asleep, or simply for recreational use. Some of the Black women respondents in this study confirm that they use over-the-counter medication, alcohol, and even marijuana to minimize the stress of workplace bullying. Given the range of substances available to manage stress, a researcher could examine which substances are the best options to manage stress from workplace bullying. Further, research could identify which substances can help Black women cope emotionally and psychologically harmful work environments.

Conclusion

Though the opening of this chapter harkened back to the heinous death of Mary Turner and her unborn child at the hands of a racist, supremist hegemonic patriarchy, her racial-motivated death provides insight into racially how Black women's health is valued in the United States. The actions of the White mob provided an unadulterated and public view on how society has disregarded the health of the Black community and Black women specifically. One of the more sensational abuses includes Johns Hopkins taking the cancer cells of Henrietta Lacks (Wolinetz & Collins, 2020). Her cancer cells were harvested and sold countless times leading to over 35,000 peer-reviewed articles and over 110,000 research articles (Năşcuţiu & Lupu, 2020). However, her family was never compensated.

Black women and health treatment

Black women's health and well-being has often been an afterthought. According to Taylor (2020), the medical community has engaged a record of "reproductive oppression" against Black women. History has revealed forced sterilization practices and heinous gynecologic experiments without anesthesia, and other medical experiments (Taylor, 2020; Washington, 2006).

In 1965, Martin Luther King Jr. stated that health disparities are the civil rights issue of the 20th century (Washington, 2006). The COVID-19 pandemic and resulting health disparities between races continue to confirm that injustice in health can be shocking and inhumane. Though society struggles to control the impact of COVID-19, cancer, diabetes, and heart disease, society, and higher education specifically, can control health-harming workplace bullying incidents through preventative measures in training and assertive policy interventions designed to stop abuse at work.

Reflective Questions and a Look Forward

Workplace bullying research has documented the deleterious impact on health for the target. This chapter also highlighted how Black women face health problems because of workplace stress. In addition to being underpaid and underappreciated, Black women disproportionately endure health issues.

1   What can organizations do to protect vulnerable populations from health problems related to workplace bullying?
2   How could organizational policy promote positive health outcomes for vulnerable employees?
3   Other countries see workplace bullying as a threat to public health. How could a group convince the US government that workplace bullying is a health issue which needs to be addressed?

Looking forward to Chapter 4, I examine Black women coaching experiences. My experiences as a former varsity volleyball player at Rutgers University and my nine years in Division-I athletic administration informed my understanding of how athletics is a challenging arena for women. The challenges are doubly so for Black women who are miscategorized and misunderstood in a competitive White male work sector.

References

American Association of University Women (AAUW) (2021). The simple truth about the gender pay gap. *Research & Data*. www.aauw.org/resources/research/simple-truth/

Anderson, K. J. (2010). *Benign bigotry: The psychology of subtle prejudice*. Cambridge University Press.

Armstrong, J. B. (2011). *Mary Turner and the memory of lynching*. University of Georgia Press.

Bailey, Z. D., Krieger, N., Agénor, M., Graves, J., Linos, N., & Bassett, M. T. (2017). Structural racism and health inequities in the USA: Evidence and interventions. *The Lancet*, *389*(10077), 1453–1463.

Bonilla-Silva, E. (2010). *Racism without racists: Color-blind racism and the persistence of inequality in the United States* (3rd ed.). Rowman & Littlefield.

Calado, R. T., & Dumitriu, B. (2013). Telomere dynamics in mice and humans. *Seminars in Hematology*, *50*(2), 165–174.

Clark, R., Anderson, N. B., Clark, V. R., & Williams, D. R. (1999). Racism as a stressor for African Americans. *The American Physiologist*, *54*(10), 805–816.

Davis, A. Y. (2011). *Women, race, & class*. Vintage.

Downs, J. (2012). *Sick from freedom: African-American illness and suffering during the civil war and reconstruction*. Oxford University Press.

DuBose, R. (2017). Compliance requires inspection: The failure of gender equal pay efforts in the United States. *Mercer Law Review*, *68*(2), 445–460.

Freire, P. (1972). *Pedagogy of the oppressed, 1968*. Trans. Myra Bergman Ramos. Herder.

Hollis, L. P. (2018). Bullied out of position: Black women's complex intersectionality, workplace bullying, and resulting career disruption. *Journal of Black Sexuality and Relationships*, *4*(3), 73–89.

Hollis, L. P. (2019a). Something to lose sleep over? Predictive analysis of Black men's and White men's Insomnia issues due to workplace bullying in higher education. *Journal of Black Sexuality and Relationships*, *5*(4), 1–19.

Hollis, L.P. (2019b). Money talks… Misogynists walk: A complex conversation on sexual harassment, race, and equal pay. In *Handbook of sexuality leadership* (pp. 207–220). Routledge.

Hollis, L. P. (2021). Mules versus (wo)men: Narrative of a Black woman modifying Maslow's theory of needs to withstand workplace bullying. *Journal of Black Sexuality and Relationships*, *7*(3), 77–92.

Hollis, L. P. (2022). *Inductive thinking 2.0 online strategies for extended case study methods and creating and ecosystem on workplace bullying.* Sage Research Methods.

Hoopsick, R. A., Vest, B. M., Homish, D. L., & Homish, G. G. (2020). Problems with social acceptance and social victimization predict substance use among US reserve/guard soldiers. *Stress and Health, 36*(3), 311–321.

Hurston, Z. N. (1937). 1990. *Their eyes were watching god.* Harper.

Johnson, C., & Smith, P. (1999). *Africans in America: America's journey through slavery.* Mifflin Harcourt.

Jones, H. L., Cross Jr., W. E., & DeFour, D. C. (2007). Race-related stress, racial identity attitudes, and mental health among Black women. *Journal of Black Psychology, 33*(2), 208–231.

Jones. J. (1985). *Labor of love labor of sorrow: Black women, work, and the family from slavery to present.* Basic Books.

Krieger, N. (2021). *Ecosocial theory, embodied truths, and the people's health.* Oxford University Press.

Krieger, N., Chen, J. T., Coull, B. A., Beckfield, J., Kiang, M. V., & Waterman, P. D. (2014). Jim Crow and premature mortality among the US black and white population, 1960–2009: An age–period–cohort analysis. *Epidemiology (Cambridge, Mass.), 25*(4), 494–504. https://doi.org/10.1097/EDE.0000000000000104

Leach, L. S., Poyser, C., & Butterworth, P. (2017). Workplace bullying and the association with suicidal ideation/thoughts and behaviour: A systematic review. *Occupational and Environmental Medicine, 74*(1), 72–79.

Lerner, G. (1977). *The female experience: An American documentary.* Oxford University Press, on demand.

Lever, I., Dyball, D., Greenberg, N., & Stevelink, S. A. (2019). Health consequences of bullying in the healthcare workplace: A systematic review. *Journal of Advanced Nursing, 75*(12), 3195–3209.

Lu, Y. K., Qiao, Y. M., Liang, X., Yao, W., Yan, Z., Wang, H. X., & Pei, J. J. (2019). Reciprocal relationship between psychosocial work stress and quality of life: the role of gender and education from the longitudinal study of the Survey of Health, Ageing and Retirement in Europe. *BMJ Open, 9*(6), e027051.

Mandziuk, R. M. (2014). "Grotesque and Ludicrous, but yet inspiring": Depictions of Sojourner truth and rhetorics of domination. *Quarterly Journal of Speech, 100*(4), 467–487.

Năşcuţiu, A. M., & Lupu, A. R. (2020). What do we owe to Henrietta Lacks? Consideration on the ethic of biobanking. *Romanian Archives of Microbiology and Immunology, 79*(1), 54–67.

Nielsen, M. B., Gjerstad, J., & Frone, M. R. (2018). Alcohol use and psychosocial stressors in the Norwegian workforce. *Substance Use & Misuse, 53*(4), 574–584.

Parker, P. S. (2004). *Race, gender, and leadership: Re-envisioning organizational leadership from the perspectives of African American women executives.* Routledge.

Rodriguez-Muñoz, A., Antino, M., Ruiz-Zorrilla, P., Sanz-Vergel, A. I., & Bakker, A. B. (2020). Short-term trajectories of workplace bullying and its impact on strain: A latent class growth modeling approach. *Journal of Occupational Health Psychology*, 1–44.

Ruscher, J. B. (2001). *Prejudiced communication: A social psychological perspective*. Guilford Press.

Sanders, J., & Newman A. (2013). Telomere length in epidemiology: A biomarker of aging, age-related disease, both, or neither? *Epidemiologic Reviews*, *35*, 112–131.

Spence Laschinger, H. K., & Nosko, A. (2015). Exposure to workplace bullying and post-traumatic stress disorder symptomology: The role of protective psychological resources. *Journal of Nursing Management*, *23*(2), 252–262.

Stannard, D. E. (1993). *American holocaust: The conquest of the new world*. Oxford University Press.

Taylor, J. K. (2020). Structural racism and maternal health among black women. *The Journal of Law, Medicine & Ethics*, *48*(3), 506–517. https://doi.org/10.1177/1073110520958875

Thompson, V. L. (1996). Perceived experiences of racism as stressful life events. *Community Mental Health Journal*, *32*(3), 223–233.

Washington, H. A. (2006). *Medical apartheid: The dark history of medical experimentation on Black Americans from colonial times to the present*. Doubleday Books.

Wolinetz, C. D., & Collins, F. S. (2020). Recognition of research participants' need for autonomy: Remembering the legacy of Henrietta Lacks. *JAMA*, *324*(11), 1027–1028. doi:10.1001/jama.2020.15936

4 Track Cleats and High Heels
Black Women Coaches Resisting Social Dominance in College Sports

Equity Exordium

I was a varsity high school and college athlete when Florence Griffith Joyner, Flo-Jo, was soaring into the zenith of her Olympic track and field career. She was strong, athletic, classy, and nontraditional with that one-legged running uniform. Coming of age, I appreciated Flo-Jo, even if she represented another sport. Studies show that women who engage in sports are less likely to deal with dating violence or domestic violence, perhaps because they found their confidence through sport (Milner & Baker, 2017).

To watch Flo-Jo's power and sophistication blaze to victory around that track gave Black girls around the globe the vision of unabashed beauty and strength. Thence, when I learned of her quote, "When anyone tells me I can't do anything ... I'm just not listening anymore," I smiled at all the times people told me I could not achieve anything. Then, I would chart my course to success and race past those naysayers. This resistance is analogous to the resistance Black women engage daily to race past those naysayers like Flo-Jo.

Background

The history of sport is built on an exclusive platform upon which men have competed to prove their virility, worthiness, expertise, and dominance. Such competition yielded a spectacle with Olympic stadiums in the fourth-century BC holding over 40,000 spectators to watch the games (Gem, 2021). The victors were memorialized as heroes who became the object of accolades and glorification in sculpture and other media. In ancient Rome, gladiatorial spectacles not only provided a platform for athletic superiority but sport was also used to control the masses with bloody amusement to distract them from challenging the ruling class

DOI: 10.4324/9781003187813-4

(Gem, 2021). The Renaissance period gave rise to men seeking an education that cultivated intellect and physicality (Gem, 2021). Athletic activities included running, riding, swimming, tennis, wrestling, fencing, and archery (until gunpowder reduced society's interest in archery) (Gems, 2014). Though women occasionally participated in riding or archery activities, historically, sport was primarily a male-dominated domain.

In the United States, sport was also a racially segregated arena. For example, professional baseball remained segregated until 1947 when Branch Rickey recruited Jackie Robinson for the Brooklyn Dodgers (Dorinson & Warmund, 2015). From 1933 through 1945, the National Football League was segregated (Oriard, 2009). Though college administrators embraced the public interest in football in the 1890s, college football was one of the last institutions to undergo desegregation. Like other organizations caught up in the raucous political wave of the 1960s, college football was also a venue grappling with racist and segregationist practices. Further, consistent defeats to northern teams with Black players convinced southern coaches to rethink integrating team rosters.

Throughout history, sport has typically been governed by men for men. Just 50 years ago, sport was by White men for White men. Contemporary numbers still reveal that while the players are increasingly Black, the coaching positions and upper administrative positions continue to be held primarily by Whites. Hence, in an arena where White men rule, and Black men had to fight their way in, Black women embrace a Herculean task to participate in sport and share in sports governance. Challenging racial and sexist norms by even attempting to participate in sport, Black women defy a complex sports culture that respects neither their race nor their gender.

Black Women in Sport

Historically, if American sport excluded Black men and excluded women, one can contemplate how society has learned to treat Black women in sport (Hollis, 2019). The answer emerges from the racist exchange in 2007 on the national radio broadcast of Don Imus, pertaining to the Rutgers women's basketball team, which had just lost in the final of a national championship to the University of Tennessee. Despite having a world-class coach in C. Vivian Stringer (coaching in the final four for Cheyney University, the University of Iowa, and Rutgers University), her team of Black women were characterized as "nappy headed hos" while Pat Summit's Tennessee team was admired as "cute" (Cookey et al., 2010). In the same radio broadcast, shock job Don Imus doubled down, commenting that the Rutgers versus Tennessee game was about "Jigaboos" versus "Wannabees"; further, his commentary compared the Rutgers women's team to the Toronto Raptors, a very aggressive men's NBA team.

Lansbury (2001) also confirmed that Black women's accomplishments are often overlooked, trivialized, or subject to racial stereotypes (Vincent, 2004). Imus's remarks are consistent with unflattering and racially disrespectful comments that the media heaps on women of color in sport. Though Imus and Lansbury were commenting 10 and 20 years ago, respectively, disparaging commentary about Black female athletes continues with the inhumanely disrespectful and racist remarks made about Serena Williams (Martin, 2018). Williams, who has trained over the years to play with unyielding power and precision, does such while breaking the norms for her sport. While other tennis stars traditionally don white garb for tennis matches, Williams wears colorful or nonconforming outfits that disrupt the expected norms in women's tennis. Perhaps one of her most compelling controversies was when she wore a black cat suit for the 2018 French Open (Love & Maxwell, 2020). Later, her cat suit was banned out of "respect [for] the game and the place" (Brown, 2018); in other words, the policing of the Black postpartum body meant she should try to conform to traditional markers of white femininity. She again disrupted patriarchal expectations when this 22-time tennis major champion gave birth to her daughter Alexis Olympia in 2017 only to return to tennis in six months and reascend to top ten status within a year (Associated Press, 2019).

Serena Williams does not stand alone in the racist/sexist intersection for women of color in sport. In 2012, 100-meter sprinter Lolo Jones faced criticism from the *New York Times*, which stated that Jones received more attention for her exotic beauty than her athletic talent (Crosby, 2016). The article from her home country just days before her Olympic finals was heartbreaking, yet aligned with the unfortunate commentary that women of color athletes face. Lansbury (2001) also documented the coverage that tennis standouts Althea Gibson and Alice Marble received. Both were African American women world-class tennis players who were categorized by their masculine style of play.

World-class sprinter Florence Griffith Joyner, aka "Flo-Jo," presented a style of resistance like Serena Williams by challenging norms through her athletic dress. While her sister-in-law counterpart, Jackie Joyner Kersee, was intensely focused on the sport without the primping and preening seen in some sprinters of color, Flo-Jo crafted an exotic image of one-legged sprinting uniforms, extra-long hair, and particularly long fingernails (Lansbury, 2014). With the world's disbelief in a sporting environment rife with doping, not only did Jackie and Flo-Jo find themselves staving off racist and sexist stereotypes, but they were also constantly defending themselves from accusations about inappropriate performance-enhancing drugs (Lansbury, 2014).

Muston and McGann (2016) note that sport remains a space in which women are miscategorized by the mainstream labels that the dominant culture imposes upon them. The media considers women as masculine and overly aggressive when they play with the same intensity and passion as their male counterparts. At times to ease tension, some women apologize for their play (Musto & McGann, 2016; Schultz, 2014). Bower et al. (2015) conducted a study of 514 women college sport administrators. Forty-one percent of respondents stated that gender stereotypes were the biggest challenge they faced in their position. Other career challenges included lack of respect, the old boys' network, and unequal pay (Bower et al., 2015).

Arguably, participation in athletics highlights the Black women's intersectionality which is based on this group of athletes being strong and skilled performers. Athleticism which is considered a male attribute can fuel stereotypes assigned to Black women athletes. Instead of being considered disciplined and proficient competitors, Black women athletes' strength and skill are transmuted to being brutish or masculine in their style of performance. In contrast, men are championed and celebrated for powerfully assertive and skilled athleticism (Musto & McGann, 2016). To combat some of their emasculating perceptions and the accompanying inaccurate trivialization (Kauer & Krane, 2006), women in college sport at times are more conscientious about their appearance and the pressure to be "more lady-like." Historically, in sport, Black women's feminine identities have come under constant scrutiny (Collins, 1990; Hollis, 1997). For Black women, who were already stereotyped as lacking feminine grace and refinement, athletic participation conjured notions of Black women athletes as animalistic.

The racialized dynamics envelope the sexualized stereotypes for Black women: an aggressive Black woman athlete who plays like a man can become suspect of sexual deviance and inappropriate masculinity (Carter-Francique & Flowers, 2013; Cookey et al., 2010; Muston & McGann, 2016). Consequently, in addition to fighting mainstream culture to achieve athletic success, Black women in sport often struggle to cultivate and maintain the identity they set for themselves in a culture that has historically denigrated their race and womanhood (Hollis, 1997).

In response, Black women in sport developed a heavy emphasis on off-the-field-appearances and reestablished their womanhood through nonathletic means (Cahn, 1994). This phenomenon continues when many women of color in sport rush to have their hair and nails done before major track meets (Hollis, 1997). Musto and McGann (2016) note in their study of 4,799 collegiate women athletes that women in sport use appearance to counter such gendered and racialized expectations. In short, they seek to conform with what Krane (2001) deemed as "hegemonic femininity," which is "constructed within a white, heterosexual, and class-based structure, and it has strong associations with heterosexual sex and romance" (Krane et al., 2004, p. 316). Put bluntly, Black women have presented themselves within traditional feminine images to avoid being labeled as lesbians. Aligning with the aforementioned researchers, Collins (2005) commented that long and straight hair along with makeup and jewelry are gender markers that signify femininity, whiteness, and heterosexuality (Hamilton, 2007; Musto & McGann, 2016). Alternatively, short hair is a nontraditional gender marker that can be taken to signify lesbianism (Hamilton, 2007; Kimport, 2012; Musto & McGann, 2016). For example, Kauer and Krane (2006, p. 48) interviewed 15 women players for their study, and a participant noted: "If you're an athlete and you have short hair, then you are definitely a lesbian. It's what people think. I swear."

Women's Work in Sport

In this historical milieu, which has traditionally been a racially exclusive environment (Widener, 2017), the dearth of coaches of color keeps underrepresented populations from securing leadership roles in collegiate sports (Martin, 2014). The sports environment is inherently male dominated, with both men and women applying stereotypes about sports leadership to the field (Walker & Sartore-Baldwin, 2013). Men are considered natural leaders, who are better at sports and therefore dominant. In contrast, when women excel in sports as players, coaches, or administrators, they violate implicit assumptions about gender-congruity (Garcia-Retamero & Lopez-Zafra, 2006). Stated otherwise, when a person presents a given gender identity (women, in this case) but seeks to excel in an area stereotypically associated with the other gender (men, in this case), then that woman is viewed as less competent or capable of performing in a workspace reserved for men. The absence of viable role models (Druckman et al., 2019; Hoch, 2011) and decades of racist and sexist media coverage sustains exclusionary and sexist norms in sport. Hegemonic masculinity, the expectation that men dominate the environment, perpetuates the exclusion of women and the sexist assumptions that plague women in sport (Kupers, 2006; Walker et al., 2017).

Additionally, Black women have encountered sex discrimination in the form of limited athletic budgets, half-hearted backing from school administrators, and sport organizations that impeded their development (Cahn, 1994, p. 119). Despite efforts to level the playing field for women in recent years, several male coaches earn more than their female counterparts or even their college presidents. Men receive more financial aid for their programs and generally are given more attention by the media (Phillip, 1993). A number of unequal pay lawsuits have been filed by women athletic personnel to address Title VII and Equal Pay violations, such as *Wiler v. Kent State University* (2021), *EEOC (on behalf of Williams) v. The George Washington University* (2020), *The United States (on behalf of Harkins) v. New Mexico State University* (2016). Notably, the hallmark world champion US women's soccer team is also in litigation for equal pay, continuing the fight for equity for women in sport.

One might consider the progress made through the 1972 Title IX legislation passed to afford women equal access to educational opportunity. In 1971, fewer than 30,000 women participated in college sport (Renelique, 2020). By the 2012–2013 athletic season, intercollegiate athletics saw a 700% increase in women's sport participation with over 200,000 women competing in intercollegiate athletics (Renelique, 2020; Theune, 2016). Title IX has fostered improvement for women in sport; nonetheless, gender inequity in hiring, fiscal commitments, and facilities persists in collegiate athletics. Indeed, "Women are experiencing a backlash for the 1972 Title IX ... as a result ... men can now apply to coach women's teams ... now women have to compete with them to coach women's teams" (Phillip, 1993, p. 24). Arguably, the preference for male coaches continues in 2021.

Racial tensions are coupled with gender inequities to create situations that diminish Black women's positions in college sport. Holloman (2015) confirmed that women of color account for less than 7% of all NCAA athletic administrators in all divisions. Additionally, while before Title IX, 90% of women's sport coaches were women, in 2019 only 41% of NCAA Division-I coaches were women (LaVoi, 2019). Ironically, though Title IX was supposed to open opportunities for women in coaching, men instead reaped the benefits, securing head coaching jobs in women's sports that were reserved for women.

Women's basketball shows progress, with 63% of head coaches being women (Rastogi & Geswein, 2019); but that progress has limited rewards for Black women, who make up over 45% of women's basketball rosters but only 11% of head coaches (Ryan, 2017). Further, only 16.1% of women's basketball assistant coaches are Black women, while 47.9% are White women (Wallick, 2018). Of athletic director positions, 76% are held by White men, 13% by Black men, 7% by White women, and only 1% by Black women (Larsen et al., 2019). Phillip's (1993, p. 25) statement from close to 30 years ago still holds true: "women have a better chance of becoming president of an NCAA institution than athletic director of that same institution."

Social Dominance Theory

In 1971, Gramsci updated the discussion regarding hegemonic manipulation and control, a social process that allows the dominant group to maintain its authority by oppressing others not in their group (Gramsci, 1971). Such oppression manifests through intolerance, homophobia, racism, sexism, nationalism, and other forms of group-level prejudice and discrimination (Sidanius & Pratto, 1999). To remain dominant, more powerful groups advocate for the status quo, a status in which they are the most powerful in society (Sidanius & Pratto, 1999; Sidanius et al., 2017), relying on the subjugation of a less powerful group. Diminished opportunities, fewer resources, and stereotypes are tools that the dominant group uses to subjugate the less powerful group (Cookey et al., 2010).

At the intersection of race, gender, and athletics, Black women in sport represent an amalgam of experiences that are central to them, but simultaneously marginalize their group in the athletic culture. The marginalization embodied by the intersection of race, gender, and athletic activity often creates an isolating experience that Black women endure while striving for athletic success. The male-dominated and patriarchal media coverage serves to further entrench racist and misogynistic stereotypes into mainstream culture, further trivializing women of color in sport (Cookey et al., 2010).

In this context, Allport's (1979) terms "in-group" and "out-group" provide a provocative vantage point from which to consider prejudice. In-group versus outgroup dynamics manifest along gender lines, along racial lines, or along any of the defining characteristics of a marginalized group. Psychologically speaking, out-group perception helps to shape in-group identity in contrast to the out-group. Hostility toward and rejection of out-groups strengthens the in-groups' sense of belonging. Allport characterizes such exclusion as a "salient need" that results in five types of rejective behavior: antilocution, avoidance, discrimination, physical attack, and extermination (Allport, 1979, pp. 48–49). Those who cling to their in-group identity do so at the risk of defining, stifling, rejecting, and possibly persecuting outgroup members by fortifying their own sense of belonging while simultaneously ostracizing people from different backgrounds.

In-group and out-group members, socialized in various ways, come together to teach in, learn, administer, and maintain the collegiate institution. Additionally, Brislin's (1993) commentary on in-groups and out-groups also provides a relevant perspective to understanding the cultural dynamics found in athletics. In-group members have positive feelings for other in-group members. This familiarity fosters positive interactions between ingroup members, yet simultaneously excludes out-group members who are considered "too different to receive in-group member attention" (Brislin, 1993, p. 181).

Regardless of an individual's position in the athletic community, those who feel part of the in-group have the propensity to feel more comfortable and less likely to feel hostility in, or isolation from, the athletic environment. According to Brislin (1993), the out-group members are kept at a distance, feeling unwelcomed and ostracized. In contrast, those welcomed into the mainstream often enjoy greater social acceptance and professional advancement than their out-group counterparts.

Allport's in-group and out-group perspective (1957) and Brislin's amalgamating perspective only consider one such group in relationship to another. Black women belong to several "out-groups" concurrently. As Hine (1993) stated, Black women experience more than the double veil that DuBois discussed. Black women endure multifaceted "fiveness": Black, American, woman, poor, and of color representing an intersectionality of marginalization. Hence, the multifaceted position leaves Black women potentially enduring the impact of multiple rejections at once. With White men as the dominant "in-group" within athletics, Black women remain on the deficit end of power. Socially subordinated by dominant groups that control social structures such as culture, education, business, and sport (Collins, 1990; Cooky et al., 2010), Black women in sport must constantly challenge magnified attempts to control their narrative and instead resist complex oppression.

Sports Structure: Division-I Versus Division-II

This study considers possible differences in Black women's experiences between Division-I and Division-II programs in NCAA amateur sports. The NCAA sports programs are divided into three categories: Division-I, Division-II, and Division-III. Division-I colleges and universities recruit student athletes and award scholarships for participation in intercollegiate sports at the highest level (Hollis, 1998). With more than 350 Division-I programs, over 6,000 student-athletes compete annually (NCAA, 2021). Division-I programs must host seven sports for each gender and at least one sport for each gender in each season (fall, winter, spring). Except for football and basketball, Division-I programs must compete exclusively against other Division-I programs. Schools in Division-I athletics make the highest level of financial commitment to sports through the quality and function of sports facilities and competition venues. Further, Division-I football and basketball have attendance requirements to maintain their Division-I status (Zullo, 2018). They must spend a minimum of $1.6 million to remain Division-I, and those schools that invest more into their athletic programs, are more competitive and visible (Haagan, 2019). As a result of the visibility, the additional resources, and personnel support, the most elite college athletes typically emerge from Division-I sports, with major championships, radio, and television coverage generating billions of dollars for Division-I colleges and universities (Zullo, 2018).

Financially, Division-I programs can potentially earn more money; they have extensive sports marketing initiatives that include significant promotion, television, and radio contracts. In many instances, colleges and universities generate revenue from student athletes' images and jerseys, along with department sponsorships from athletic apparel and beverage corporations. In contrast, Division-II sports do not have the same financial benefits or obligations. Division-II programs, which are traditionally at smaller or private colleges, do not commit to the same financial obligations as their Division-I counterparts and are only required to host five sports for men and five sports for women (Zullo, 2018). Unlike Division-I, they offer fewer scholarships and tend to commit to a regional competition, which incurs lower travel expenses than those entailed by national competition schedules (Difference, 2021). Division-II sports do not have the same media relations and sports information budgets. Unlike Division-I programs, which flood their general student body with information to attend games, Division-II programs do not engage in this type of attendance development. Comparatively, Division-I programs have revenue sharing across conference, but Division-II athletic programs keep the revenue that they generate.

The distinctions between Division-I and Division-II potentially contribute to how Black women coaches and administrators are treated. The extreme financial element and media attention for Division-I sports means that athletics is packaged as a commodity to be bought and sold to fans and the media. In this context, Division-I sports generate billions of dollars annually (Rovell, 2018). History has proven time and again that the hegemonic entitlement in our culture is often driven by money. Therefore, one can expect that Black women in Division-I programs may face more pressure to conform to hegemonic expectations and experience more intense restrictions to please paying fans.

The Study

This research aims to examine the social pressure that Black women coaches and team coordinators feel to conform with the dominant culture's traditional expectations of femininity. Previous studies note that women in athletics carefully think about their clothing, hair, and other gendered markers to counter stereotypical assumptions about women and sport. These expectations for Black women potentially include acquiescing to standards of white beauty in hair, makeup, and dress. Further, one might consider that there is increased pressure for Division-I personnel when compared to Division-II personnel, because Division-I programs presumably have increased patriarchal influence due to increased media exposure, financial tensions, and heightened competition.

Data Collection

In the fall of 2020, I invited Black women head coaches, associate head coaches, assistant head coaches, and coordinators from Division-I and Division-II sports to complete a survey exploring racialized and gendered expectations in appearance. The women were recruited primarily from women's basketball, volleyball, soccer, softball, and track using publicly available emails found on athletic department websites. To secure a sample for this analysis, I recruited Black women head coaches, associate head coaches, assistant head coaches, and coordinators from Division-I and Division-II sports programs. I used the list of Division-I sports conferences from the NCAA website and visited every athletic department's website, compiling emails from women's basketball, women's track and field, women's volleyball, and other sports. I repeated the same process with Division-II sports conferences. Once a distribution list had been compiled, I obtained IRB approval, and women from the distribution list were invited to participate and sent a link to the survey.

Research Method

The recruitment led to a sample of 106 Black women coaches and coordinators. The central research questions were as follows:

RQ1:   What is the difference in racialized/gendered expectations to comply with mainstream appearance between Division-I programs and Division-II programs?

H1:   *Black women coaches and personnel face more pressure at the Division-I level when compared to the Division-II level.*

RQ2:   How do Black women coaches perceive their acceptance in their respective sports programs?

Sample

Of the 106 Black women who responded to the survey, 77% were from Division-I programs and 23% were from Division-II programs. Most were from women's basketball (48.56%). The rest were from volleyball (24.5%) and other sports (26.5%) such as track and field, soccer, tennis, and swimming.

Data Analysis

To address the first research question ("What is the difference in racialized/gendered expectations to comply with mainstream appearance between Division-I programs and Division-II programs?"), I filtered the responses into Division-I and Division-II. A total of $n = 106$ Black women coaches and sports personnel from Division-I and Division-II schools replied to the question. Then, I examined if Black women coaches and personnel were pressured to maintain a certain "feminine" or mainstream appearance. The survey question was "Do you feel pressure or an expectation to wear 'more feminine' clothes during competition (skirts, stockings, heels, dangle earrings, blouse with cleavage)?" Women who responded that they had this pressure at least once an academic year were coded "1" for yes. Women who reported pressure every other year or less were coded "2" for no (see Table 4.1).

Therefore, hypothesis **H1** for this study (*"Black women coaches and personnel face more pressure at the Division-I level when compared to the Division-II level"*) is not accepted, $X^2 = (2, n = 106) = 1.09, p < .05$.

Table 4.1 Black women coaches pressured to conform in appearance (*n* = 106)

	Yes	No	Total
Division 1 CT	32	49	81
Division 1 Exp CT	29.8	51.2	81
Division 2 CT	7	18	25
Division 2 Exp CT	9.2	15.8	25

Qualitative Content Analysis

At the conclusion of the survey, participants were asked to leave a comment about their coaching experience; 39 did so. From those 39 remarks, five themes emerged: (1) stereotype of angry Black woman; (2) gender discrimination; (3) more Black women are needed in administration; (4) team mammy; (5) lucky to have a good experience.

Theme #1: Stereotype of Angry Black Woman

Most Black women are caught in a double bind when it comes to displaying assertive behavior. Even justified anger feeds into the angry Black woman stereotype, while silence means complicity. Ironically, in athletics, which is a male-dominated arena, Black women are still criticized for behaviors that do not align with traditional expectations of demure womanhood. Participants expressed the following views and sentiments regarding this aspect of their experience:

* "Some people don't understand my passion. I feel that they take it as me being angry or mean or tough, but it is the way that I show that I care."
* "I am at a PWI, so I get the angry Black female and combative narrative more than anything."
* "I was labeled as the 'angry Black girl,' which in turn silenced me."
* "If I was a man, my assertiveness would be looked at as 'She gets the job done and has high expectations.' But instead, it's labeled as aggressive."

Theme #2: Gender Discrimination

It can be expected that an analysis of Black women's work experiences should uncover discrimination, because Black women sit at the intersection of several Title VII protected classes. The experiences of the respondents are congruent with the reasonable assumption about discrimination. Black women coaches often felt overlooked or forced to comply with traditional standards of white womanhood, commenting on this as follows:

- "I have experienced a pervasiveness of racist and gender bias and sexism, stifling the professional growth of female coaches, manifest in misidentification, differential treatment, tokenism, isolation, and motherhood."
- "I have faced discrimination from my own White players."
- "I think my experiences as a Black woman is [sic] different from other races. A change in my then, I am perceived as aggressive."
- "It's exhausting. We are held to a different standard and marginalized in so many ways."

Theme #3: More Black Women Are Needed

Research shows that some very capable women do not enter athletics or coaching because of the racist and sexist dynamics in male hegemonic environments. While not a universal solution, additional Black women in leadership positions may assist with other women's careers. Women respondents hoped for such but recognized as well that the masculine and competitive nature of their work environment did not automatically mean that women would support other women.

- "There needs to be more of us especially in male sport."
- "Would love to see more women athletic directors."
- "I think it's very difficult to find allyship: especially as a woman of color. Even the women in the profession fight against each other to get the 'one' position delegated for women."
- "I've never been privy to what influence SWAs (Senior Women Administrators) have outside of handling issues with women's programs."

Theme #4: Team Mammy

Black women coaches not only noted that men could coach women's teams more than women coach men's teams, but they also noted that men often wanted to operate above the issues collegiate young women experience. In such scenarios with a male head coach, women associates and assistant coaches were relegated to the position of "team mammy."

Some respondents reported that men wanted leadership positions but did not want to deal with personal issues. Hence, the Black woman on staff was left exclusively to play the role of emotional nurse:

- "If I am the only female on a staff, there is an expectation to take care of 'girl problems' and tasked with being the only one to converse and work with student athletes."
- "I strongly resent the implication that I am the 'team mom.'"
- "Many times, I have been forced to confront my African American student athletes about severe or minor problems because my White male coach refused to handle their issues or address race issues."

Theme #5: Lucky to Have a Good Experience

Black women serving in a supportive environment were aware that they were lucky or blessed to work in such an environment. While interacting with other women coaches, Black women coaches in this sample who recognized a good work environment knew they were the exception and not the rule.

- "I am fortunate to not have sexual pressures and have worked for head coaches with great integrity."
- "My school does well. I have never been made to feel super uncomfortable beyond men calling me 'sweetie' and [saying things like] 'You should smile more.'"
- "I have been fortunate to feel secure and supported in my work environment."

Discussion

The world of American sports has historically been dominated by White men. In turn, the insurgence of Black men is a relatively new phenomenon since the 1960s desegregation movement. In this context, Black women are disavowed, diminished, and disrespected by the hegemonic social order meant to maintain the patriarchal status quo. One could argue that Black women can be bullied into silence when they do not conform to traditional expectations (Hollis, 2018). As Gitlin (1980) and Crosby (2016) posit, hegemonic structures limit human potential and competition to maintain dominance for the ruling population.

By maintaining exclusionary values, the hegemonic dominant culture does two things simultaneously. First, those outside of its "in-group" remain shunned, as is the case of Black women. Second, by repressing competition, the hegemonic culture risks mediocrity. Instead of embracing diversity and the natural competition that inspires productive advancement, when the hegemonic culture eliminates competition instead of benefiting from it, that hegemonic culture is lulled into mediocrity (Oluo, 2020). Entitlement erases the advancement available through competitive innovation. Hence, in diminishing the authentic voices of Black women in sport, the hegemonic environment only diminishes its own development and evolution for the preference of maintaining traditional entitlement.

Recommendations

Several women in the study commented that they felt isolated and misunderstood. According to this sample, the pressures for Black women working in sport environments that are not culturally competent seem similar regardless of Division-I or Division-II status. To alleviate the confirmed alienation felt by many Black women, the following steps are recommended.

1   Develop a national mentorship program for Black women entering sports administration and coaching. While operating within a culture of hegemonic masculinity, Black women would benefit from connections with other Black women coaches and sports personnel across the nation. Other specialized professional fields have organizations for Blacks, such as the Association of Black Cardiologists (ABC), the Association of African American Museums (AAAM), and the Organization of Black Aerospace Professionals (OBAP). However, there appears to be no professional organization for Black women sports personnel.

2   Develop capacity-building programs. Just as several organizations have functions to support people of color with grant writing, research, and publishing, a national organization can also support Black women sports personnel. A summer three-day event to guide Black women rising in sports administrators would not only support the capacity for Black women to progress in sports environments but also develop networks that Black women can use throughout their careers.

3   If men of any race are serving as head coaches of any women's team, they should have formal training in working with young women. The NCAA could require that coaches have six credits, that is, two three-credit women's studies courses. A third class dealing with female late adolescent development should also be a

requirement. If coaches do not have these courses, the respective colleges and universities should have courses in these topics that coaches can take so they are better prepared to support their female student-athletes.

Reflective Questions and a Look Forward

With close to 15 years of experience as an administrator and varsity athlete, I was startled by the finding in this study that mentioned the "team mammy." Too often, Black women are underpaid or harassed but expected to address the less appealing job functions. These expectations in sport diminish Black women and teach an entire team of young women that Black women are only subordinate figures.

1   What can be done to shift Division-I and Division-II sports culture to be more inclusive for Black women?
2   Athletics is a fast-paced and competitive field by nature. How can one determine what workplace bullying is and what are appropriate cultural norms in athletics?
3   What kind of programs or systems could be implemented to mentor Black women seeking careers in athletics?

Looking forward to Chapter 5, I address an age-old problem of colorism. People have embraced the notion that those with lighter skin are more attractive and more intelligent throughout the world. Unfortunately, this misnomer hurts people with darker complexions when they are treated poorly and denied opportunities because of their skin. Subsequently, this final chapter examines colorism as a compelling factor for Black women targeted by workplace bullying.

References

Allport, G. (1979). *The nature of prejudice*. Addison-Wesley.
Associated Press. (2019). Serena Williams in the top 10 after giving birth. *USA Today*. www.usatoday.com/story/sports/tennis/2019/02/18/serena-williams-back-in-top-10-after-giving-birth/39075847/
Bower, G. G., Hums, M. A., & Grappendorf, H. (2015). Same story; different day: Greatest challenges of women working in intercollegiate athletic administration. *International Journal of Sport Management, Recreation & Tourism*, *19*, 12–39.
Brislin, R. (1993). *Understanding culture's influence on behavior*. East-West Center.

Brown, S. M. (2018, September). Serena Williams catsuit ban exposes racism in sports. *Washington Informer.* https://login.proxy.libraries.rutgers.edu/login?url=https://www.proquest.com/newspapers/serena-williams-catsuit-ban-exposes-racism-sports/docview/2103515531/

Cahn, S. (1994) *Coming on strong: Gender and sexuality in twentieth century women's sports.* Harvard Press.

Carter-Francique, A. R., & Flowers, C. L. (2013). Intersections of race, ethnicity, and gender in sport. In E. A. Roper (Ed.), *Gender relations in sport, teaching gender* (pp. 73–93). Sense Publishers. doi:10.1007/978-94-6209-455-0_5

Collins, P. H. (1990). *Black feminist thought: Knowledge, consciousness, and the politics of empowerment.* Routledge.

Cooky, C., Wachs, F. L., Messner, M., & Dworkin, S. L. (2010). It's not about the game: Don Imus, race, class, gender and sexuality in contemporary media. *Sociology of Sport Journal, 27*(2), 139–159.

Crosby, E. D. (2016). Chased by the double bind: Intersectionality and the disciplining of Lolo Jones. *Women's Studies in Communication, 39*(2), 228–248.

Differences. (2021). Divisional differences and the history of multidivision classification. NCAA Organization. www.ncaa.org/about/who-we-are/membership/divisional-differences-and-history-multidivision-classification

Dorinson, J., & Warmund, J. (2015). *Jackie Robinson: Race, sports and the American dream.* Routledge.

Druckman, J. N., Howat, A. J., & Rothschild, J. E. (2019). Political protesting, race, and college athletics: Why diversity among coaches matters. *Social Science Quarterly, 100*(4), 1009–1022.

Garcia-Retamero, R., & Lopez-Zafra, E. (2006). Prejudice against women in male-congenial environments: Perceptions of gender role congruity in leadership. *Sex Roles, 55*, 51–61. https://doi.org/10.1007/s11199-006-9068-1

Gems, G. R. (2014). *Boxing: A concise history of the sweet science.* Rowman & Littlefield.

Gems, G. R. (2021). *Sport history: The basics.* Routledge.

Gitlin, T. (1980). *The whole world is watching.* University of California Press.

Gramsci, A. (1971). *Selections from the prison notebooks* (Hoare, Q. & Nowell Smith, G., Ed. and Trans.). International.

Haagen, P. (2019). Sports in the courts: The NCAA and the future of intercollegiate revenue sports. *Judicature, 103*(2), 1–11.

Hamilton, L. (2007). Trading on heterosexuality college women's gender strategies and homophobia. *Gender & Society, 21*(2), 145–172. doi:10.1177/0891243206297604

Hine, D.C. (1993). In the kingdom of culture: Black women and the intersection of race, gender, and class. In G. Early (Ed.) Lure and Loathing. Penguin (pp 337–351)

Hoch, D. (2011). Coaches as role models. *NFHS Coaching Today.* http://old.nfhs.org/CoachingTodayContent.aspx?id=8709

Hollis, L. P. (1997). The ultimate triple jump: The psychosocial, historical, and current dynamics affecting African American female athletes' identity and success. *Academic Athletic Journal, 12*(1), 11–19.

Hollis, L. P. (1998). *Equal opportunity for student-athletes: Factors influencing student-athlete graduation rates in higher education.* Boston University.

Hollis, L. P. (2018). The ironic interplay of free speech and silencing: Does workplace bullying compromise free speech in higher education? *AAUP Journal of Academic Freedom, 9*, 1–15.

Hollis, L. P. (2019). Lessons from Bandura's Bobo Doll experiments: Leadership's deliberate indifference exacerbates workplace bullying in higher education. *Journal for the Study of Postsecondary and Tertiary Education, 4*, 85–102.

Hollomon, N. (2015). *Perceived barriers for ethnic minority females in collegiate athletic careers: Barriers report ethnic minority females.* National Collegiate Athletic Association.

Kauer, K. J., & Krane, V. (2006). "Scary dykes" and "feminine queens": Stereotypes and female collegiate athletes. *Women in Sport and Physical Activity Journal, 15*(1), 42–52.

Kimport, K. (2012). Remaking the white wedding? Same sex wedding photographs' challenge to symbolic heteronormativity. *Gender & Society, 26*(6), 874–899. doi:10.1177/0891243212449902

Krane, V., Choi, P. Y. L., Baird, S. M., Aimar, C. M., & Kauer, K. J. (2004). Living the paradox: Female athletes negotiate femininity and muscularity. *Sex Roles, 50*, 315–329.

Kupers, T. A (2005) Toxic masculinity as a barrier to mental health treatment in prison. *Journal of Clinical Psychology, 61*(6), 713–724. https://doi.org/10.1002/jclp.20105

Lansbury, J. H. (2001). "The Tuskegee flash" and "the slender Harlem Stroker": Black women athletes on the margin. *Journal of Sport History, 22*, 235–252.

Lansbury, J. H. (2014). *A spectacular leap: Black women athletes in twentieth-century America.* University of Arkansas Press.

Larsen, L. K., Fisher, L., & Moret, L. (2019). The coach's journal: Experiences of Black female assistant coaches in NCAA Division I Women's basketball. *Coach, 3*, 632–658.

LaVoi, N. M. (2019, April). *Head coaches of women's collegiate teams: A report on seven select NCAA Division-I institutions, 2018-19.* Minneapolis, MN: The Tucker Center for Research on Girls & Women in Sport. www.tuckercenter.org

Love, J., & Maxwell, L. C. (2020). Serena Williams: From catsuit to controversy. *International Journal of Sport Communication, 13*(1), 28–54.

Martin, L. (2014). The Black athlete and the post-racial myth. In L. L. Martin (Ed.), *Out of bounds: Racism and the Black athlete* (pp. 3–28). Praeger.

Martin, L. L. (2018). Double fault: Serena Williams and tennis at the intersection of race and gender. *Western Journal of Black Studies, 42*, 88–97.

Milner, A. N., & Baker, E. H. (2017). Athletic participation and intimate partner violence victimization: Investigating sport involvement, self-esteem, and abuse patterns for women and men. *Journal of Interpersonal Violence*, *32*(2), 268–289. https://doi.org/10.1177/0886260515585543

Musto, M., & McGann, P. J. (2016). Strike a pose! The femininity effect in collegiate women's sport. *Sociology of Sport Journal*, *33*(2), 101–112.

NCAA (National Collegiate Athletic Association) (2021). Our Division-I Story. www.ncaa.org/sports/2021/2/16/our-division-i-story.aspx

Oluo, I. (2020). *Mediocre: The dangerous legacy of white male power.* Hachette.

Oriard, M. (2009). *Bowled over: Big-time college football from the sixties to the BCS era.* Chapel Hill, NC: University of North Carolina Press.

Philip, M. (1993). An uneven playing field: Gender factor still a hurdle for women. *Black Issues in Higher Education*, *10*(20), 24–25.

Rastogi, A., & Geswein, K. (2019). Percentage of female NCAA Division 1 women's basketball coaches by conference. *HerHoopStats.* https://medium. com/her-hoop-stats/percentage-of-female-ncaa-division-i-womens-basketb all-coaches-by-conference-a442afd49428

Renelique, S. M. (2020). *The underrepresentation of women of color in senior management athletic administration at NCAA Division I institutions.* Arkansas State University.

Rovell, D. (2018). NCAA tops $1 billion in revenue during 2016–2017 school year. *ESPN College Sports.* www.espn.com/college-sports/story/_/id/22678 988/ncaa-tops-1-billion-revenue-first

Ryan, S. (2017). College sports needs more women–and women of color– in coaching ranks. *Chicago Tribune.* www.chicagotribune.com/sports/ct-wom ens-college-coaching-diversity-ryan-spt-0419-20170417-column.html

Sidanius, J., Cotterill, S., Sheehy-Skeffington, J., Kteily, N., & Carvacho, H. (2017). Social dominance theory: Explorations in the psychology of oppression. In C. G. Sibley & F. K. Barlow (Eds.), *The Cambridge handbook of the psychology of prejudice* (pp. 149–187). Cambridge University Press. https://doi.org/10.1017/9781316161579.008

Sidanius, J., & Pratto, F. (1999). *Social dominance: An intergroup theory of social hierarchy and oppression.* Cambridge University Press.

Theune, F. (2016). The shrinking presence of Black female student-athletes at historically Black colleges and universities. *Sociology of Sport Journal*, *33*(1), 66–74.

United States Equal Employments Opportunity Commission (EEOC) (on behalf of Williams) v. George Washington University. 502 F. Supp. 3d 62 (D.D. 2020)

United States (on behalf of Harkins) v. New Mexico State. No. 16-CV-911-JAP-LF (D.N.M) 2018)

Vincent, J. (2004). Game, sex and match: The construction of gender in British newspaper coverage of the 2000 Wimbledon championship. *Sociology of Sport Journal*, *21*, 435–456.

Walker, N. A., Schaeperkoetter, C., & Darvin, L. (2017). Institutionalized practices in sport leadership. In L. J. Burton & S. Leberman (Eds.), *Women in sport leadership: Research and practice for change* (pp. 33–46). Routledge.

Wallick, K. N. (2018). Underrepresentation of women in sports leadership: Stereotypes, discrimination, and race. *Student Publications*, 687. https://cupola.gettysburg.edu/student_scholarship/687

Widener, D. (2017). Race and sport. In R. Edelman & W. Wilson (Eds.), *Oxford handbook of sports history* (pp. 462–476). Oxford University Press.

Zullo, R. (2018). Sports marketing & publicity efforts in Division II intercollegiate athletics. *The Sport Journal, 21.*

5 Color Coded Intersections

Workplace Bullying, Colorism, and Its Impact Along Race and Gender Lines

Equity Exordium

American communities witness this colorism problem daily. Too often, music videos and movies telegraph the preference for light-skinned people. In a world where dark people were castigated and vilified, people with lighter skin experienced more acceptance. However, the color-struck phenomena, or colorism, fosters degradation and misgivings that accompany skin tone bias.

While dark-complected people were denied employment, housing, and common respect even within their families, light-skinned people who were passing for White experienced existential threats as well. To be in a White society, passing as White, could result in disastrous consequences for the person passing. The light-skinned/dark skin controversies continue to plague the Black community. Nella Larsen's (2001) remarks from her book *Passing* elucidate the treachery for those using their skin tone to transcend color lines. "She wished to find out about this hazardous business of 'passing,' ... not entirely strange, perhaps, but certainly not entirely friendly" (Larsen, 2001, p.186)

Background

Larsen's words are simply on a historical continuum that grapples with the privilege that accompanies skin tone. In Upper Egypt's Aswan region, the dark-complexioned Nubians were referred to as "the golden people" because of their renowned wealth in ivory, incense, ebony, and gold (Eisler, 1949; Hassan, 2007). However, in the United States, particularly dark people have been subjected to what Steele (2016) categorizes as the pejorative phrase "blue-black," which signifies the deep melanin of dark-complexioned people (Snell, 2017). Steele further posits that such slurs are hegemonic controls transmitted in intragroup discourse to

DOI: 10.4324/9781003187813-5

suppress those whose features diverge from European standards (Steele, 2016). In short, regardless of the location or the historical moment, society has subscribed to colorism on a global scale. Dixon and Telles (2017) document that White supremacist views and color prejudice have infiltrated Asian communities, Latin/Hispanic communities, and Black/ African American communities to categorize people in a stratum of social acceptability and superiority.

Colorism is proven to hurt Blacks, as those with lighter skin are often favored in education and employment. History shows that colorism in the American context traces back to slavery as a control mechanism that disenfranchises those of African descent and the mixed-race children emerging from slavery (Dixon & Telles, 2017; Monk; 2014; Norwood; 2013). Exclusionary tactics used by both Blacks and Whites included the paper bag test, in which Blacks who were darker than a brown paper bag were excluded from some social clubs, sororities, and fraternities. The blue vein test served similar purposes, assessing people based on whether their veins could be seen beneath the skin of their inner forearms (Dixon & Telles, 2017; Geyen, 2014). The blue vein test was the foundation of exclusive Blue Vein Societies, which were recognized as a Black/ African American aristocracy, members of which were more educated and earned higher wages. While not operating in contemporary society, Blue Vein Societies proliferated colorized expectations for Black/African Americans that still influence social expectations of race and color. Just as the vestiges of slavery still inform American society and communities across the globe in terms of assumptions about race and social hierarchy, color also remains a seemingly indelible marker of social status.

The widespread phenomenon of colorism, which several societies use to exclude darker-complexioned people from equity and opportunity, will be examined as a central element in workplace bullying. Workplace bullying behaviors exploit a power differential between someone with more power and an employee with less power. The abuse, which is often learned organizational behavior, occurs over some time, with an escalating nature in which the target is left in a deficit position (Hollis, 2019; Zapf et al., 2003). This study confirms that skin tone bias is directly linked to lower wages and diminished educational opportunities. In turn, these deficits can contribute to darker employees being relegated to less powerful positions in the workplace and thereby becoming more susceptible to abusive workplace bullying. After examining several ways in which dark-complexioned Blacks/African Americans are persecuted because of their skin color, this chapter will discuss how colorism may be directly linked to workplace bullying for Black/African American women.

Colorism in US History

Skin tones from the lightest alabaster albino to the darkest ebony have been judged by multiple cultures across various historical moments. Historically, in the United States, an individual's race was determined by the mother's condition with the one-drop rule (Goldsmith, Hamilton, & Darity, 2007; Khanna, 2010). With American slavery came racial mixing between White indentured servants and Black slaves (Williamson, 1980). From the fear of corrupting the White race, state legislators in Maryland and Virginia passed laws to prohibit miscegenation. Despite the laws, mixed-race children were born. Khanna (2010) noted that early colonists faced a dilemma on how to categorize the mixed-race children, from which the one-drop rule emerged.

The one-drop rule held that if the mother was Black or part Black, which means her children were part Black, then that one drop of Black blood, regardless of the child's skin color or features, would render that offspring Black, and a slave. In the social hierarchy among slaves, dark-skinned Blacks were considered inferior and assigned harsh work in the field, while lighter-skinned slaves often worked inside and were even given a skill beyond manual labor (Neal & Wilson, 1989; Lincoln, 1968; Wade, Romano & Blue, 2004). Consequently, lighter-skinned slaves received better living conditions, better clothes, better shoes, and educational instruction, while darker-skinned slaves were consigned to more physically arduous labor and social marginalization (Egbeyemi, 2019). This is borne out by Kerr's (2006) finding that, during the Reconstruction years of the late 1880s, 60% of mulattoes could read, while only 20% of brown and darker-skinned Blacks could read (as cited in Egbeyemi, 2019). In fact, dark-skinned Blacks were at times banned from church because that church painted a door a shade of light brown, rejecting potential parishioners whose skin was darker than the door (Frazier, 1963; Monk, 2021). From the inception of the United States, the social mores were that if one is Black, one should stay back.

Skin color has continued to be an issue of contention in workspaces. For example, Goldsmith et al. (2007) note the social construction of whiteness, giving those with fairer skin greater access to resources, jobs, and housing. This led Goldsmith et al. to hypothesize that the wage gap for Blacks/African Americans becomes more pronounced as skin color deepens. Their Multi-City Study of Urban Inequity confirmed that lighter-skinned Blacks earned approximately 10% to 12% more than darker-skinned Blacks. Hersch's (2018) longitudinal study of 4,363 immigrants also revealed that skin color was directly linked to wage disparity, of 16%–25%, becoming more prevalent from light skin to dark skin.

Researchers continue to confirm that skin color is associated with better economic and educational success (Keith & Herring, 1991; Hughes & Hertel, 1990). Wade, Romano, and Blue (2004) built their colorism analysis on previous studies that link beauty, light skin, and enhanced social and financial status. Society-associated whiteness with beauty, civility, and virtue, while blackness was viewed as vile, dirty, and ugly (Hill, 2002; Steele, 2016). Dixon and Telles (2017) confirm that mixed-race Blacks, or mulattoes, had greater access to a skilled position after slavery; therefore, they had greater social mobility. Further, mulattoes tended to marry other mulattoes, hence propelling their light-skinned household past the earning power of their undereducated darker-skinned counterparts (Dixon & Telles, 2017; Herring et al., 2007).

By using Feingold (1992) and Eagly, Ashmore, Makhijani, and Longo (1991), researchers such as Wade et al. (2004) confirmed such financial benefits in contemporary America when they studied 107 college students in a gender-balanced sample to confirm that lighter-skinned Blacks/African Americans experienced better employment experiences. Those who were lighter were considered more attractive, even beautiful. Such perceived beauty by the employer contributed to higher salaries. As a result, fair skin is associated with stronger earning power and higher socioeconomic status (Wade et al., 2004). In short, light-skinned men are more likely to have more robust economic and social status.

Within the historical background of colorism, darker-complexioned Blacks face greater exposure to discipline that exclude them from their communities. For example, in a longitudinal study of over 6,400 students, Blake et al. (2017) found that darker-complexioned Black girls faced suspension twice as often as White girls, yet this statistic did not hold true for light-complexioned Black girls. Suspension, which is on the slippery slope to expulsions, rendered dark-complexioned girls more likely to endure exclusionary discipline and join the fast track to juvenile justice and adult incarceration (Morris, 2016).

Health and Tone

Several researchers have noted that stress exacerbates health problems (Boen, 2020; DuBois, [1899] 1995; Harnois et al., 2019; Monk, 2021). With darker-skinned Blacks/African Americans subjected to lower paying jobs, less access to education, and more attention from the justice system, it can be inferred that darker individuals are more likely to have more stress-related health issues. Using data from the National Survey of American Life, Monk (2021) found that skin tone discrimination is related to heart problems and issues relating to cardiometabolic rate. Further, Monk's study confirmed that discrimination is related to body aches and pain; the problem is exacerbated when the discrimination occurs within the same racial group. Additionally, color bias within the Black community is significantly related to morbidity among Blacks. Crutchfield et al. (2017) confirmed that those with darker complexions are more susceptible to depression and are at greater risk of substance abuse, a typical coping mechanism for people facing stress and anxiety (Crutchfield et al., 2017; Hollis, 2020b; Smith-Bynum et al., 2008; Veestra, 2011). Stated another way, Blacks who face rejection and discrimination within their own racial groups experience more stress and associated health problems than if facing the expected rejective prejudice from Whites.

Gendered Issues and Colorism

Dark-skinned women often are criticized or shamed for darker skin and simultaneously deemed less attractive with the accompanying thicker lips, thicker bodies, and broader noses (Dixon & Telles, 2017; Hughes & Herring, 2013; Rosario, Minor, & Rogers, 2021; Ross, 2020). Hegemonic ideas about beauty congruent with European skin color and features serve to subjugate women of color whose appearance does not align with that standard. Within this context, lighter-skinned women are more visible in the media, with some of the earliest paradigms of this trend being Lena Horne and Eartha Kitt (Hollis, 2020a). For example, Lena Horne, a light-skinned African American, graced the cover of *Ebony Magazine* multiple times as the quintessential Black woman (Williams, 2009). Though Horne was a civil rights advocate in her own right, her image for decades recast the picture of Black womanhood to minimize connection with the oversexed Jezebel and Sapphire and the presumably unattractive and overly domesticated dark-skinned mammy (Brown, White-Johnson, & Griffin-Fennell, 2013; Sewell, 2013; Williams, 2009). While *Ebony Magazine* was a media revolution as a mainstream magazine by and for the Black/African American community, the images in its pages reinforced the preferences for light skin and European features (Glenn, 2008).

Additionally, colorism affects Black men and interferes with their livelihoods. For example, a longitudinal study of 4,340 men confirms that taller and darker-skinned Black men earn less. This factor was not mitigated by education, as those dark-skinned people who excelled beyond high school also earned less than their light-skinned counterparts (Devaraj, Quigley, & Patel, 2018). Darker skin tones are also directly related to police stops, arrests, and sentencings (Burch, 2015; Monk, 2018; White, 2014).

The same rejective patterns are prevalent in police killings, in which darker-complexioned men are more likely to be murdered by the police. A short list of Black men gunned down by police over the past decade includes George Floyd in Minneapolis, Minnesota, May 2020; Ahmaud Arbery, Brunswick, Georgia, February 2020; Dennis Plowden Jr., December 2017, Philadelphia, Pennsylvania; Walter Scott, North Charleston, South Carolina, April 2015; Eric Gardner, New York, New York, July 2014; Michael Brown, Ferguson, Missouri, August 2014; and Trayvon Martin, Sanford, Florida, February 2012. All of these Black men brought down by racist police were tall and dark-complexioned.

Theoretical Frame: Modified Allport

Allport (1957) clearly outlined the nature of prejudice in chronicling the levels of rejection an in-group would perpetrate against an out-group. Whether the in-group is a family system, a sports team, or a community, such groups can engage in punitive behaviors when rejecting others. In Allport's spectrum, which starts with antilocution and continues through extermination, I include bullying as a rejective behavior. Figure 5.1 illustrates my original modification of Allport's spectrum of rejective behaviors.

In Allport's progressive series of aggressive and rejective behaviors, bullying plausibly falls after discrimination. Other studies note that bullying can be derived from masked animus or suppressed prejudice (Hollis, 2021). Whether a gang of schoolyard children or a wolfpack group of workplace peers, a more powerful group can violently reject the target or out-group member. Such dynamics are confirmed in the

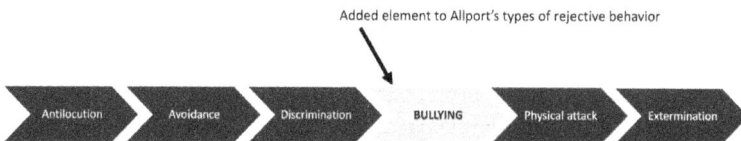

Figure 5.1 Modified Allport series of rejective behaviors.

aforementioned brief list of Black men killed by the police. In the most severe cases, bullying was on the continuum to suicide and death (Brailovskaia, 2020; Hollis, 2017).

In this application of colorism, the dominant group is White, and those with lighter skin and European features are closer to the dominant White group in appearance. Smith-McLallen, Johnson, Dovidio, and Pearson (2006) discuss skin tone bias with society's perception that light and white are good, desired, and positive; yet in converse, dark and black brings a negative perception of being linked to evil, bad, and sullied (Devaraj, Quigley, & Patel, 2018). White is angelic, holy, and Godlike, even in a religious context, while dark represents sins and demons. Following this logic, the whiter and lighter in-group would reject the darker out-group. In my analysis, bullying is inserted into Allport's rejective behaviors spectrum.

With the historical examples of colorism that confirm that society does not accept or appreciate blackness with the same enthusiasm as whiteness, I consider a previous study (Hollis, 2020a) that found that darker-complexioned Blacks/African Americans are more likely to experience workplace bullying. Further, previous studies confirmed that women, and Black women specifically, are also more likely to encounter workplace bullying when compared to their male counterparts (Hollis, 2018). Building on the findings of these two previous studies, I hypothesize in this analysis that dark-complexioned Black/African American women, who are at the intersection of discrimination on the basis of race, gender, and color, will be more likely to face workplace bullying when compared to dark-complexioned men, light-complexioned men, and light-complexioned women.

Research Methods

Data Collection

During the fall of 2020, I disseminated a 12-question survey via SurveyMonkey™. The respondents were recruited through their LinkedIn contact information. The recruitment email that I disseminated encouraged people to forward the link to the survey to their friends. The SurveyMonkey platform estimated that respondents needed three minutes to complete the 12-question survey. When I conduct survey research, I usually send an initial recruitment email and three additional reminders in the following nine weeks. In this case, I achieved the target sample with only the first email and one reminder, which indicates substantial interest in the study.

I have developed over 15 survey-based research projects in the past seven years. My process includes engaging a comprehensive literature review and then developing survey questions. Before dissemination, the survey was beta-tested by a diversity inclusion officer, a sociologist, and a professor of women's studies. As a member of the African American community, it seemed to me that I would be likely to have some preconceived bias about colorism; however, the survey questions that appear in the appendix were neutral to support the validity of the study. As this survey-based study was about colorism in the Black/African American community, only responses from members of the Black/African American community were used in the data analysis; therefore, 100% of the sample identifies as African American/Black. In addition, to address colorism, I asked participants to identify with a skin complexion.

The respondents were recruited through my LinkedIn account regardless of occupation. Recruitment resulted in *n* = 304 participants. To investigate colorism, a color palette of skin colors was embedded in the survey: Russet (*n* = 109), Peru (*n* = 72), Fawn, (*n* = 40), Apricot (*n* = 29), and Navajo White (*n* = 5). The color palette is entitled *Real Skin Tones* from SchemColor (www.schemecolor.com/).

I used Krippendorf's (1980, 1989) qualitative content analysis to address the second research question. Researchers Elo and Kyngs (2008) and Harwood and Garry (2003) noted that this research method was developed in the 19th century to examine religious texts, hymns, and sermons. Through this process, a researcher can take formerly unmeasurable elements and distill them into measurable themes. Consequently, the qualitative content analysis process allows researchers to uncover new knowledge from patterns found in language and pictures. Through this process, the researcher initially cultivates a sample. The sample contributes sentences, phrases, and comments, which are then recategorized into salient themes.

Research Questions

To further investigate the intersectional dynamic in colorism along gender lines, I used the following research questions for this investigation. This question has two hypotheses.

RQ1   *Which Black/African American colleagues, dark women, light women, dark men or light men, are more likely to face workplace bullying?*

H1   African American/Black women with darker skin complexions are more likely to report workplace bullying than lighter African Americans/Blacks.

H2   African American/Black women with darker skin complexions are more likely to report workplace bullying than all African American men.

RQ2   *How does workplace bullying affect Blacks'/African Americans' workplace experience and health?*

Findings

I used chi-square analysis to address the first research question, which considered color and gender simultaneously in incidents of workplace bullying for Blacks/African Americans. The findings align with a previous study in which color alone was a compelling factor in workplace bullying (see Table 5.1).

Therefore, **H1** ("African American/Black women with darker skin complexions are more likely to report workplace bullying than the other groups of African Americans/Blacks") is not accepted at a statistically significant level (X^2 (2, n = 304) = 23.88, $p \le$ .01).

To address the second research question—"How does workplace bullying affect Blacks/African Americans' workplace experience and health?"—Table 5.2 lists the frequencies at which Blacks/African Americans report various health problems. The most common problem related to the stress of workplace bullying is insomnia (35.14%). Additionally, 13.18% reported increased alcohol use to cope with bullying. In response to workplace bullying, 21.96% sought a coach or counseling for support.

Table 5.1 Colorism and workplace bullying, gender, and color (n = 304)

	1 = Yes	*2 = No*	*Total*
DK men Count	55	23	78
DK men Exp Count	48.8	29.3	78
DK women Count	106	46	152
DK women Exp Count	95	57	152
LGT men Count	9	9	18
LGT men Exp Count	11.3	6.8	18
LGT women Count	20	36	56
LGT women Exp Count	35	21	56

Table 5.2 Workplace bullying impact on health (*n* = 296)

I have trouble sleeping because of workplace bullying.	35.14%	*n* = 104
I take more sleep medication to sleep as a result of workplace bullying.	8.11%	*n* = 24
I have increased my alcohol intake to cope with workplace bullying	13.18%	*n* = 39
I have sought a counselor or coach to cope with workplace bullying.	21.96%	*n* = 65
I have taken sedatives (prescription or over the counter) to deal with workplace bullying.	7.09%	*n* =21
I experienced a decreased interest in physical intimacy with my partner due to workplace bullying.	10.14%	*n* = 30
I have had suicidal ideation because of workplace bullying.	3.04%	*n* = 9
Have not experienced workplace bullying.	32.09%	*n* = 95

From the *n* = 296 sample who answered an open-ended question on this topic, *n* = 70 were used in a qualitative content analysis. I used a qualitative content analysis to uncover themes in the open-ended remarks. These respondents' comments identified notable behaviors such as relying on prayer to cope with the stress, or that respondents experienced addictive behaviors with alcohol or gambling to take their minds off the abuse. Moreover, the four following themes emerged in respect of the association between health problems and workplace bullying.

Theme #1: Disengagement

Though not a health issue, disengagement occurs when employees feel psychologically unsafe or unstimulated by their work. In an emotionally and psychologically abusive workspace, respondents commented that they disengaged from the work:

"I was hesitant to do my job."

"I have become less engaged with the team or person cause [sic] the bullying."

"Doing only what is required to do my job, nothing more."

Theme #2: Stress/Anxiety

Unsurprisingly, workplace bullying leads to increased stress on the job. Respondents recognize that this stress was related to health issues:

"Rash from stress."
"Take anxiety/stress meds."
"Gained weight from the stress."
"Gastro intestinal issues, migraines, chest pains and back pains."

Theme #3: Anger

Given the persistent unfair treatment, many respondents also were angered by the constant abusive bullying. Potentially, this anger is informed by theme #1 about employee disengagement.

"I became more and more angry over all."
"I speak my truth. I push back!"
"Feelings of anger and anxiety."
"I was more angry and defensive."

Discussion

This printed page does not visually capture the technical kaleidoscope of hues from which human beings live. In this historical moment, society is facing existential threats in the form of global warming, the COVID-19 pandemic, and extended gun violence (Allan, 2007; Esposito & Finley, 2014; Simchon et al., 2021). As noted by Crenshaw (2019), an Obama phenomenon visited in which color blindness and a post-racial position were embraced. However, fickle American society resurrected overt discrimination with the 45th presidential administration (Hollis, 2021). With these problems facing our global population, our global society needs to transcend historic and contemporary colorism and instead focus on our tasks at hand. The talent embodied in people of color regardless of skin tone can pave the way for cures and climate control. Yet, while our communities remain beholden to European standards of beauty that connote power and privilege, we limit ourselves by not allowing talent from all populations to emerge.

Diversity management and research about organizational productivity prove that diverse teams are more productive teams (Hamilton, Nickerson & Owan, 2012; Rock, Grant, & Grey, 2016). Various backgrounds and experiences, which often reside in diverse body types and shades, can propel society forward and solve the ills facing our communities. To further understand and eradicate colorism, the following are recommended in research, policy, and practice.

Research

The Black/African American community is not the only community facing color discrimination.

1 Additional studies about workplace bullying could examine gender and colorism in Lantix, indigenous, and Asian communities.
2 As this study confirmed that dark-complexioned men are the most likely to face workplace bullying, future research could consider more in-depth analysis regarding colorism and its impact on men's health.
3 Though this study has confirmed that colorism hurts dark-complexioned men and women in the workplace, researchers can also examine how colorism affects Blacks/African Americans in other sectors such as college, real estate, and commerce.

Practice

1 Because colorism is an extension of long-standing social structures that perpetuate colorist norms from slavery, Blacks/African Americans may benefit from counseling to minimize color bias in our community.
2 Workplaces along with fraternities and sororities can hold programs to educate their community about the discriminatory ills in colorism.
3 Organizations, especially minority-serving organizations, can further investigate if their employees feel mistreated not only due to gender but also due to colorism.

Policy

1 Just as organizations have training about sexual harassment and racial discrimination, organizations can also include colorism as a topic for diversity training.
2 Complaint forms typically ask about the nature of someone's complaint, such as race, gender, and retaliation. Colorism should be added as a ground for formal complaints.

3   Organizations should explicitly recognize colorism in their Title VII antidiscrimination policies and explicitly note colorism as an issue separate from racism.

Conclusion

Diversity and inclusion efforts typically underestimate colorism and the discrimination that results from it. Through such exclusion, people who experience colorism often do not have a voice when claiming that the color of their skin is a contributing factor in the abuse they endure.

Surprisingly, these findings identified dark-skinned men as being more likely to face bullying when compared to dark-skinned women. Previous data have revealed that men are the least likely to be bullied (Salin & Hoel, 2013). Therefore, I expected that men, who still have privileged regardless of their skin, would face less workplace bullying. The analysis of this sample proved otherwise. However, based on this sample, the intersection of male gender and dark skin is more threatening to mainstream society and thus leads to the increased rates of bullying observed among this group.

Reflective Questions and Intersectionality

When I conducted my first study on colorism, a participant wrote, "What? This is still a thing?" The unfortunate answer is "yes," because our society still embraces the notion that whiteness alone is good, pure, innocent, and privileged. However, we miss the invaluable kaleidoscope of intellectual thought and expression which fortify our respective global communities.

1   If Title VII prohibits colorism as a civil rights violation, why is it an underused charge? How can that change?
2   If one develops a policy, how can they create processes that honor all contributions regardless of employees' diverse skin tones?
3   How has colorism manifested in various workplaces such as education, athletics, and business? What are some examples?

The findings from all five chapters confirm Freier's (1972) perspective about oppressors changing their strategies. The overt harassment and discrimination from the Jim Crow era are more subtle. Though this remark infers that workplace bullying is another form of discrimination, the truth is anyone can face bullying in any work environment for various reasons. Nonetheless, those with minimal power and resources tend to be most susceptible to abuse, including workplace bullying. The disenfranchised and disposed along racial, gendered, and color lines become disenchanted and disillusioned about actualizing the constitutional promise of equal protection under the law.

References

Allan, B. B. (2017). Second only to nuclear war: Science and the making of existential threat in global climate governance. *International Studies Quarterly*, *61*(4), 809–820. https://doi.org/10.1093/isq/sqx048

Allport, G. (1957). *The nature of prejudice*. Perseus Books.

Blake, J. J., Keith, V. M., Luo, W., Le, H., & Salter, P. (2017). The role of colorism in explaining African American females' suspension risk. *School Psychology Quarterly*, *32*(1), 118–130. http://dx.doi.org/10.1037/spq0000173

Boen, C. (2020). Death by a thousand cuts: Stress exposure and black–white disparities in physiological functioning in late life. *The Journals of Gerontology: Series B*, *75*(9), 1937–1950.

Brailovskaia, J., Ujma, M., Friedrich, S., & Teismann, T. (2020). Thwarted belongingness and perceived burdensomeness mediate the association between bullying and suicide ideation. *Crisis: The Journal of Crisis Intervention and Suicide Prevention*, *41*(2), 136–140. doi:10.1027/0227-5910/a000596

Brown, D. L., White-Johnson, R. L., & Griffin-Fennell, F. D. (2013). Breaking the chains: Examining the endorsement of modern Jezebel images and racial-ethnic esteem among African American women. *Culture, Health & Sexuality*, *15*(5), 525–539.

Burch, T. (2015). Skin color and the criminal justice system: Beyond black-white disparities in sentencing. *Journal of Empirical Legal Studies*, *12*(3), 395–420.

Crenshaw, K. W. (Ed.). (2019). *Seeing race again: Countering colorblindness across the disciplines*. University of California Press.

Crutchfield, J., Fisher, A., & Webb, S. L. (2017). Colorism and police killings. *Western Journal of Black Studies*, *41*, 81–91.

Devaraj, S., Quigley, N. R., & Patel, P. C. (2018). The effects of skin tone, height, and gender on earnings. *PLoS ONE*, *13*(1), 1–22.

Dixon, A. R., & Telles, E. E. (2017). Skin color and colorism: Global research, concepts, and measurement. *Annual Review of Sociology*, *43*, 405–424. https://doi.org/10.1146/annurev-soc-060116-053315

Du Bois, W. E. B. [1899] 1995. *The Philadelphia negro: A social study*. University of Pennsylvania Press.

Eagly, A. H., Ashmore, R. D., Makhijani, M. G., & Longo, L. C. (1991). What is beautiful is good, but …: A meta-analytic review of research on the physical attractiveness stereotype. *Psychological Bulletin*, *110*(1), 109.

Egbeyemi, A. (2019). Shedding light on colorism: How the colonial fabrication of colorism impacts the lives of African American women. *Journal of Integrative Research & Reflection*, *2*(2), 14–25.

Eisler, R. (1949). Metallurgical anthropology in Hesiod and Plato and the date of a "Phoenician lie." *Isis, 40*(2), 108–112. https://doi.org/10.1086/349033

Elo, S., & Kyngs, H. (2008). The qualitative content analysis process. *Journal of Advanced Nursing, 62*(1), 107–115.

Esposito, L., & Finley, L. L. (2014). Beyond gun control: Examining neo-liberalism, pro-gun politics and gun violence in the United States. *Theory in Action, 7*(2), 74–103. doi:10.3798/tia.1937-0237.14011

Fiengold, A. (1992). Good-looking people are not what we think. *Psychological Bulletin, 111*(2), 304.

Franklin, F. (1963). *The Negro Church in America.* Shocken Books.

Freire, P. (1972). *Pedagogy of the oppressed.* 1968. Trans. M. B. Ramos. Herder.

Geyen, D. (2014). Blue vein society/paper bag test. In L. H. Cousins (Ed.), *Encyclopedia of human services and diversity* (Vol. 1, pp. 155–157). SAGE.

Glenn, E. N. (2008). Yearning for lightness: Transnational circuits in the marketing and consumption of skin lighteners. *Gender & Society, 22*(3), 281–302.

Goldsmith, A. H., Hamilton, D., & Darity, W. (2007). From dark to light: Skin color and wages among African-Americans. *Journal of Human Resources, 42*(4), 701–738.

Hamilton, B. H., Nickerson, J. A., & Owan, H. (2012). Diversity and productivity in production teams. In *Advances in the economic analysis of participatory and labor-managed firms.* Emerald Group Publishing Limited.

Harnois, C. E., Bastos, J. L., Campbell, M. E., & Keith, V. M. (2019). Measuring perceived mistreatment across diverse social groups: An evaluation of the Everyday Discrimination Scale. *Social Science & Medicine, 232*, 298–306.

Harwood, T.G., & Garry T. (2003). An overview of content analysis. *The Marketing Review, 3*, 479–498.

Hassan, F. (2007). The Aswan High Dam and the International Rescue Nubia Campaign. *African Archaeological Review, 24*(3/4), 73–94.

Herring, C., Keith, V., & Horton, H. D. (2004). *Skin deep: How race and complexion matter in the "color-blind" era.* University of Illinois Press.

Hersch, J. (2018). Colorism against legal immigrants to the United States. *American Behavioral Scientist, 62*(14), 2117–2132. https://doi.org/10.1177/0002764218810758

Hill, M. E. (2002). Skin color and the perception of attractiveness among African Americans: Does gender make a difference? *Social Psychology Quarterly, 65*(1), 77–91.

Hollis, L. P. (2017). Turn the other cheek: HBCU students' reaction to collegiate bullying. *Journal of Black Sexuality and Relationships, 3*(4), 35–60.

Hollis, L. P. (2018). Bullied out of position: Black women's complex intersectionality, workplace bullying, and resulting career disruption. *Journal of Black Sexuality and Relationships, 4*(3), 73–89.

Hollis, L. P. (2019). Lessons from Bandura's Bobo Doll experiments: Leadership's deliberate indifference exacerbates workplace bullying in higher education. *Journal for the Study of Postsecondary and Tertiary Education, 4*, 85–102.

Hollis, L. P. (2020a). Brown and bullied around: The relationship between colorism and workplace bullying for African Americans/Blacks. In K. Woodson (Ed.), *Colorism then, now, & tomorrow: Refining a global phenomenon with implication for policy, research and practice* (pp. 158–173). Fielding University Press.

Hollis, L. P. (2020b). Her beleaguered libido: Black women's decreased desire and self-medicating reaction to workplace bullying. *Journal of Black Sexuality and Relationships, 6*(4), 99–114.

Hollis, L. P. (2021). A tribe called Trump, motivation behind the education line: Why some people of color voted for the bully-in-chief? *Taboo, 20*(3), 164–177.

Hughes, M., & Hertel, B. R. (1990). The significance of color remains: A study of life chances, mate selection, and ethnic consciousness among Black Americans. *Social Forces, 68*(4), 1105–1120.

Hughes, N. M., & Herring, C. (2013). Fairness on the job: Skin tone, the beauty myth, and the treatment of African American women at work. In *Reinventing race, reinventing racism* (pp. 177–197). Brill.

Keith, V. M., & Herring, C. (1991). Skin tone and stratification in the Black community. *American Journal of Sociology, 97*(3), 760–778.

Kerr, A. E. (2006). *The paper bag principle: Class, colorism, and rumor and the case of Black Washington.* University of Tennessee Press.

Khanna, N. (2010). "If you're half black, you're just black": Reflected appraisals and the persistence of the one-drop rule. *The Sociological Quarterly, 51*(1), 96–121.

Krippendorff, K. (1980). *Content analysis: An introduction to its methodology.* SAGE.

Krippendorff, K. (1989). Content analysis. In E. Barnouw, G. Gerbner, W. Schramm, T. L. Worth, & L. Gross (Eds.), *International encyclopedia of communication* (Vol. 1, pp. 403–407).

Larsen, N. (2001). The complete fiction of Nella Larsen: Passing. *Quicksand and the Stories.* Anchor.

Lincoln, C. E. (1968). Color and group identity in the United States. *Color and Race*, 249–263.

Monk, E. P. (2014). Skin tone stratification among black Americans, 2001–2003. *Social Forces, 92*(4), 1313–1337.

Monk, E. P. (2018). The color of punishment: African Americans, skin tone, and the criminal justice system. *Ethnic and Racial Studies.* doi:10.1080/01419870.2018.1508736

Monk, E. P. (2021). Colorism and physical health: Evidence from a national survey. *Journal of Health and Social Behavior, 62*(1), 37–52.

Morris, M. (2016). *Pushout: The criminalization of Black girls in schools.* The New Press.

Neal, A. M., & Wilson, M. L. (1989). The role of skin color and features in the Black community: Implications for Black women and therapy. *Clinical Psychology Review, 9*(3), 323–333.

Norwood, K. J. (2013). *Color matters: Skin tone bias and the myth of a postracial America*. Routledge.

Rock, D., Grant, H., & Grey, J. (2016). Diverse teams feel less comfortable—and that's why they perform better. *Harvard Business Review, 95*(9), 22–25.

Rosario, R. J., Minor, I., & Rogers, L. O. (2021). "Oh, you're pretty for a dark-skinned girl": Black adolescent girls' identities and resistance to colorism. *Journal of Adolescent Research, 36*(5), 501–534. https://doi.org/10.1177/07435584211028218

Ross, K. (2020, June 4). Call it what it is: Anti-blackness. *New York Times*, Opinion. www.nytimes.com/2020/06/04/opinion/george-floyd-anti-blackness.html

Salin, D., & Hoel, H. (2013). Workplace bullying as a gendered phenomenon. *Journal of Managerial Psychology, 28*(3), 235–251. http://dx.doi.org/10.1108/02683941311321187

Sewell, C. (2013). Mammies and matriarchs: Tracing images of the Black female in popular culture 1950s to present. *Journal of African American Studies, 17*(3), 308–326. https://doi.org/10.1007/s12111-012-9238-x

Simchon, A., Turkin, C., Svoray, T., Kloog, I., Dorman, M., & Gilead, M. (2021). Beyond doubt in a dangerous world: The effect of existential threats on the certitude of societal discourse. *Journal of Experimental Social Psychology, 97*. https://doi.org/10.1016/j.jesp.2021.104221

Smith-Bynum, M., Best, C., Barnes, S. L., & Burton, E. T. (2008). Private regard, identity protection, and perceived racism among African American adolescents. *Journal of African American Studies, 12*, 142–155.

Smith-McLallen, A., Johnson, B.T., Dovidio, J.F., & Pearson, A.R. (2006). Black and white: The role of color bias in implicit race bias. *Social Cognition, 24*, 46–73.

Snell, J. (2017). Colorism/neo-colorism. *Education, 138*(2), 205–209.

Steele, C. K. (2016). Pride and prejudice: Pervasiveness of colorism and the animated series proud family. *The Howard Journal of Communications, 27*(1), 53–67. https://doi.org/10.1080/10646175.2015.1117028

Veestra, G. (2011). Mismatched racial identities, colourism, and health in Toronto and Vancouver. *Social Sciences & Medicine, 73*, 1152–1162.

Wade, T. J., Romano, M. J., & Blue, L. (2004). The effect of African American skin color on hiring preferences 1. *Journal of Applied Social Psychology, 34*(12), 2550–2558.

White, K. (2014). The salience of skin tone: Effects on the exercise of police enforcement authority. *Ethnic and Racial Studies, 38*(6), 993–1010.

Williams, M. E. (2009). "Meet the real Lena Horne": Representations of Lena Horne in Ebony Magazine, 1945–1949. *Journal of American Studies, 43*(1), 117–130.

Williamson, J. (1980). *New people: Miscegenation and mulattoes in the United States*. The Free Press.

Zapf, D., Einarsen, S., Hoel, H., & Vartia, M. (2003). Empirical findings on bullying in the workplace. Bullying and emotional abuse in the workplace. *International Perspectives in Research and Practice, 103125*.

Afterword

I started studying workplace bullying from a universal perspective. As a scholar emerging from Rutgers University in 1990, I pursued Black women's writings and pleased in retrospect that my desire to collect Black scholarship has left me with a small library of what is now called Critical Race Theory. I digress. Though I sought out a cutting-edge Black feminist scholarship in the 1990s, I was advised to stay universal in my writing. Some of my mentors, not all, cautioned me against focusing on "Black projects." I should not pigeonhole my scholarship.

In the last 12 years, my research started with that universal perspective, looking at workplace bullying as a general, class-free, status-free problem. The truth is, anyone and everyone can face bullying if they are subjected to unchecked power in a tyrannical organization. While one or two bullies may initiate the problem, the organization enables bullying when it refuses to intervene (Hollis, 2021a). The leadership action or inaction sets the tone for acceptable behavior and can enable employee persecution that leads to career disruption and extensive health problems (Hollis, 2017). As noted in Bandura's social psychological research, people learn acceptable behavior from the authority in the environment (Bandura, Ross, & Ross, 1961; Hollis, 2019) If the leader intervenes and admonishes bad behavior, bystanders soon learn to change that behavior.

I am a Black woman scholar whose education has encouraged me to read in concert with or against issues of race and gender in literature, history, and sociology. The mere terms of Black studies, ethnic studies, and women's studies connote an "othering" of the very essential persona that embodies my thinking. Emerging scholars from the decades that I was in school in the late 1980s and 1990s faced the question of being a mainstream or "other" scholar. Mainstream thinking meant race and gender were tertiary and potentially exotic sidebar discussions. For example, those mainstream readings from my literary training were the canon, a body of work produced by the "DWIMS" as we called it, the dead White men of Shakespeare, Chaucer, Milton, Marlow, etc. My training presented a choice to be at the center or reside in the margins of academic thought, away from the canon.

This same dynamic evolved from my dissertation (Hollis, 1998). I started the study about Division I student-athletes thinking I was conducting a race-blind study. However, race emerged again when I analyzed data about men's football, men's basketball, and women's basketball. I was uncustomarily silent with my dissertation committee while I grappled with the supposedly color-blind data staring me in the face. Echoing the words of Derek Bell (Bell, 1992; Clark, 1995), race is permanent; it is always there. My attempt to ignore race and gender in my early research was futile and somewhat irresponsible. To answer the data in my dissertation, I added an additional analysis to address the impact of race in the data. After graduation, perhaps instead of grappling with race and gender scholarship and as an emerging researcher in the late 1990s, I entered university administration.

After 16 years as a higher education administrator, I reentered rigorous academic research with a different perspective and into a slightly different academic research culture. Despite the push from people for me to remain mainstream, my administrative experiences confirmed that race and gender were ubiquitous elements, spoken or not. Bell (1995) was right; race is there always. Clark is right (1995) intersectionality is permanent.

Employees' power, privilege, and pay were directly associated with race and gender. Demographic positions of race and gender were not just elephants in the room; they were the room. These demographic markers inform who is on search committees or accreditation boards. Race and gender inform who is appointed to a position rather than competing in a national search. The further one ascended in their careers, the smaller the room, meaning the fewer opportunities along racial and gender lines. Though I saw such dynamics firsthand regardless of which college or university I worked, the data in educational research confirm the diminished leadership opportunities for women, people of color, and especially for those in the intersecting position as a woman of color. Nonetheless, when returning to a research career, my initial studies on workplace bullying continued where my 1990s training left off. The first major publication on workplace bullying that I wrote, *Bully in the Ivory Tower* (2012), was a color-blind treatise from this vantage point that universal and color blind research would prevail. My initial assumptions were validated as the *Chronicle of Higher Education,*

University Business, higherjobs.com, and *Inside Higher Education* covered the publication. However, I am since pleased to be disabused of this "universal approach" notion.

Much of my research is instrument/survey-based, hence congruent with my doctoral training at Boston University. A standard part of survey-based research is to collect demographic information. This simple universal standard brought me right back to the racial and gendered elements of workplace bullying that I had witnessed firsthand in my administrative career. Race and gender are ALWAYS an issue, good or bad. Color-blind approaches are incomplete approaches, especially with our society evolving as a majority–minority culture. Vulnerable populations tend to be from the margins taught to me in the 1990s. Yet, the data also elucidated that class, power, and privilege associated with racial and gendered social constructs are driving forces on who is afforded respectful dignity on the job.

Central to my approach in examining race and gender in workplace bullying research is through Paulo Freire (1972), who stated that the oppressor does not just stop but will seek other means to deliver that same oppression. Hence, with the 1964 Civil Rights Laws, discriminatory colleagues learned that hanging nooses, glaring swastikas, and girlie calendar pinups are no longer viable tactics in discriminatory intimidation. Such overt markers of prejudice and discrimination dissolved, but the intent still festers. Though all workplace bullying is not driven by racist and sexist animus, someone with racist or sexist animus can use bullying tactics to exact pain and anxiety on their targets without invoking a Title VII charge. The data reveal such time and again.

The continuing evolution that any scholar experiences has led me to this text in which I examine how the inextricably linked personas of race, gender, and skin tone infiltrate work, health, and sport. Though Black women are over 53% of the Black workforce in America (Bureau of Labor Statistics, 2019), the academy still is deficient in understanding Blacks or women, let alone Black women. Regardless of how we couch it, as gendered racism, racist sexism, or intersectionalism, Black women's experiences remain understudied and underappreciated.

Why might this intellectual journey be significant to workplace bullying research?

So often I have heard women and people of color claiming a status-free station, seeking to sit in a universal position of acceptance. No one is bashing acceptance. Sense of belonging is a basic human need (Noltemeyer et al., 2021). But regardless of where a Black woman goes, there she is, Black and woman (Blackshear & Hollis, 2021). No universal approach or intellectual exercise can undo self-evident and indelible truths in racial and gendered social constructions.

Workplace bullying may occur because that bully is insecure, incompetent, narcissistic, or corrupt. There is plenty wrong with a bully who chooses to prop themselves upon the backs of others with impunity. Nonetheless, the target must know, race and gender are part of the equation. Black women are mobbed by other women more so than White female counterparts (Hollis, 2021b). I have witnessed Black women bully other Black women because the target is smarter, has a bigger house, or has a handsome spouse. In one instance, one Black woman called another a "big baby" in a heated discussion of unequal pay. Certainly, the higher paid name-caller did not invoke such infantilization with her White male colleagues but reserved such bully-style persecution for someone who looked like herself. Black women have reported their hyper consciousness for not being labeled that "angry Black woman," despite the total justification she had to lift her voice to protest unfair treatment.

The desire to "best" another in a competitive work environment stem from the beginning of work itself. Competitive dog-eat-dog tactics, especially in competitive academic environments, aid some colleagues in eliminating challengers. In my consulting visits over the past 15 years, I have been privy to egregious workplace behaviors, such as a colleague urinating in another's soda and leaving it for the target in the fridge. One scientist remarked that her lab specimens were destroyed when the bully knowingly unplugged the incubator before a holiday weekend. The result was devasting to the target's seven-figure grant project. Perhaps the worst example occurred during a campus conversation where a very public sexual assault precipitated major upheavals among the women faculty. However, the most powerful woman administrator in the room, who had her own teenaged daughter, forcefully shut down the conversation by blurting out, "I don't see what the big deal is – sometimes people just get raped." Shock and awe cannot capture the slack-jawed reaction in the group to hear such a callous remark from a woman.

These are just a few examples of bullying strategies designed to suppress real or perceived challenges. As noted throughout the international literature, workplace bullies emerge across gender and race lines, resulting in organizational, emotional, and psychological damage. Nevertheless, Black women, given the historical and social disadvantages, must remain focused and diligent, not only in our work but also in crafting an effective resistance against workplace tyranny.

To trope the Hull et al.'s (1982) title, I maintain that all the bullies are enabled; all the targets are hurt, but some of us must remain brave.

Leah P. Hollis, EdD
Senior Research Associate
Samuel Dewitt Proctor Institute
Rutgers University
May 2022

References

Bandura, A., Ross, D., & Ross, S. A. (1961). Transmission of aggression through imitation of aggressive models. *The Journal of Abnormal and Social Psychology*, *63*(3), 575–582.

Bell, D. (1992). *Faces at the bottom of the well: The permanence of racism*. Basic Books, a member of the Perseus Books Group.

Blackshear, T., & Hollis, L.P. (2021) Despite the place, cant escapes gender and race: Black women's faculty experience at PWIs and HBCUS. *Taboo: The Journal of Culture and Education*. 28–50.

Bureau of Labor Statistics. (2019). Black women made up 53% of the Black labor force in 2018. *U.S. Department of Labor, The Economics Daily*. www.bls.gov/opub/ted/2019/black-women-made-up-53-percent-of-the-black-labor-force-in-2018.htm

Clark, L. D. (1995). A critique of professor Derrick A. Bell's thesis of the permanence of racism and his strategy of confrontation. *Denver University Law Review*, *73*, 23.

Freire, P. (1972). *Pedagogy of the oppressed*. 1968. Trans. M. B. Ramos. Herder.

Hollis, L. P. (1998). *Equal opportunity for student-athletes: Factors influencing student-athlete graduation rates in higher education*. Boston University.

Hollis, L. P. (2012). *Bully in the ivory tower: How aggression and incivility erode higher education*. Patricia Berkly.

Hollis, L. P. (2017). Workplace bullying II: A civilizational shortcoming examined in a comparative content analysis. *Comparative Civilizations Review*, *77*(77), 90–104.

Hollis, L. P. (2019). Lessons from Bandura's Bobo Doll experiments: Leadership's deliberate indifference exacerbates workplace bullying in higher education. *Journal for the Study of Postsecondary and Tertiary Education*, *4*, 85–102.

Hollis L. P. (2021a). *Human resource perspectives on workplace bullying in higher education: Understanding vulnerable employees' experiences*. Routledge.

Hollis, L. P. (2021b). An unfair fight: Black women's additional risk: Facing "mobbing" in higher education. Ed (Hollis L.P.) In *Human resource perspectives on workplace bullying in higher education: Understanding vulnerable employees' experiences*. Routledge.

Hull, G. T., Hull, A. G., Bell-Scott, P., & Smith, B. (Eds.). (1982). *All the women are white, all the blacks are men, but some of us are brave: Black women's studies*. Feminist Press.

Noltemeyer, A., James, A. G., Bush, K., Bergen, D., Barrios, V., & Patton, J. (2021). The relationship between deficiency needs and growth needs: The continuing investigation of Maslow's theory. *Child & Youth Services*, *42*(1), 24–42.

Index

For Product Safety Concerns and Information please contact our EU
representative GPSR@taylorandfrancis.com
Taylor & Francis Verlag GmbH, Kaufingerstraße 24, 80331 München, Germany